EXECUTIVE EDITOR
Natalie Earnheart

CREATIVE TEAM
Jenny Doan, Natalie Earnheart, Christine Ricks, Tyler MacBeth, Mike Brunner, Lauren Dorton, Jennifer Dowling, Dustin Weant, Jessica Toye, Kimberly Forman, Denise Lane, Grant Flook, Cathleen Tripp

EDITORS & COPYWRITERS
Nichole Spravzoff, Camille Maddox, Julie Barber-Arutyunyan, Hillary Doan Sperry, Lora Kroush

SEWIST TEAM
Jenny Doan, Natalie Earnheart, Courtenay Hughes, Carol Henderson, Cassandra Ratliff, Janice Richardson

PRINTING COORDINATOR
Rob Stoebener

PRINTING SERVICES
Walsworth Print Group
803 South Missouri
Marceline, MO 64658

CONTACT US
Missouri Star Quilt Company
114 N Davis
Hamilton, MO 64644
888-571-1122
info@missouriquiltco.com

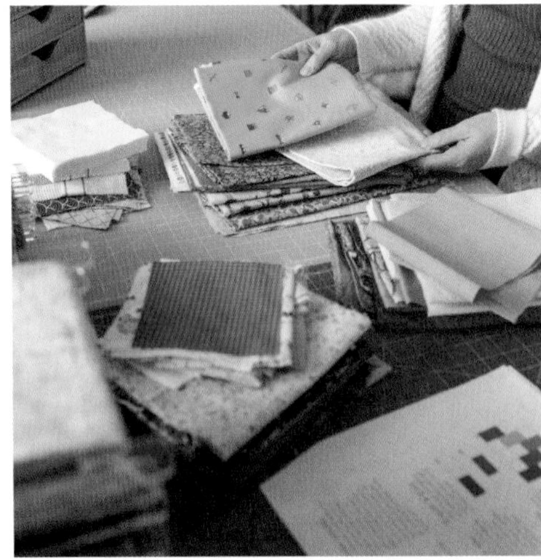

6 **OVERCOMING CREATIVE BLOCKS**

If creativity is so rewarding, why is it difficult to incorporate into our lives? Learn all about why we often struggle to find our creative spark and complete more projects in 2022!

30 **THE QUILTING MARINE**

People often find quilting in times of need to help them through difficult situations—that's how Mark Darrell, The Quilting Marine, first discovered his love for quilting.

50 **WHAT IS A QUILT WORTH?**

The value of a quilt is deeply embedded in every stitch, much more than the sum of its parts. Read on to discover why a quilt has inherent artistic, emotional, and cultural value.

76 **COMMUNITY CONNECTION**

Since 2008, Little Dresses for Africa has been improving the lives of children all across the continent of Africa. It all started with simple dresses made of pillowcases and has become so much more.

14 BOARDWALK

Do you enjoy long, romantic walks to the sewing room? This lovely Boardwalk quilt is the perfect scrappy project to get you in a sewing mood.

22 LAYERED DIAMONDS

What's even better than diamonds? Layers and layers of them! Add extra sparkle to this lovely holiday quilt design with tiny secondary diamonds right at the points of larger diamonds.

34 EMOTION SHADOW BLOCK

Build your emotion crumb blocks with The Quilting Marine from fabric scraps. Then, see how clever sashing casts beautiful shadows.

56 JUST WING IT

When you're looking for a quilt to help your imagination take flight, go ahead and just wing it. This quilt's definitely for the birds!

62 LAKEVIEW TERRACE

Is there anything more relaxing than lounging lakeside as the water laps gently on the shore? Capture the movement of the serene waters with this lovely quilt.

68 LOTS O' LUCK TABLE RUNNER

Stitch up a lucky table runner just in time for St. Patrick's Day in stunning shades of blue and green. It's sure to give you more good luck than a four-leaf clover!

84 CONVERSATION HEART PILLOWS

Remember those cute pastel candy hearts we used to eat on Valentine's Day? Now you can make a cozy pillow filled with love that looks just like those classic confections.

90 FABRIC CHECKERBOARD

King me! Create a fun fabric checkerboard the whole family will love that includes storage for your pieces in clever zipper pouches. It can also be used for portable games of chess.

96 TREE FARM TABLE RUNNER

Picking out the perfect Christmas tree is a beloved holiday tradition and this darling table runner features rows and rows of tiny pine trees, just like our favorite tree farm.

102 BUTTERFLY HOUSE

Covered in a kaleidoscope of fluttering patchwork butterflies, this charming Butterfly House quilt is sure to attract plenty of snuggles.

A note from Jenny

Dear Quilters,

Whenever a new year begins, it's natural to look back on our efforts during the previous year and wonder how we might improve. But I want to add a gentle word of caution about setting goals with the right intent. Beginning with a feeling of shame that we were unable to meet our goals from the previous year will only cause further pain and hinder our ability to actually improve. Instead, begin with a clean slate. Allow yourself to bravely start fresh and feel the excitement of possibility. Revel in it. Soak it in. As Henri Matisse famously said, "Creativity takes courage."

Believe that in your soul you are a creative being. We all have that desire somewhere within us and it's crucial to express it. So, how can we unleash greater creativity in the new year? Here are a few tips I have gathered up for encouraging greater creativity: *Get rid of the guilt.* Move forward with intent and know your efforts are good enough. *Prioritize playing and resting.* These two are the fuel for creativity. *Practice being calm.* Literally breathe before you decide how to feel. Instead of reacting before you have the bigger picture, collect the facts and make a decision. It's key in a world where circumstances can change so quickly! *Let go of self-doubt and "supposed-tos."* You are the one who decides what is essential in your life. And finally, my favorites—*Laugh more, sing more, and dance more!* Cue up your favorite tune and do a kitchen boogie when you're in need of inspiration. It works wonders.

Thank you for showing up just as you are. Quilters, you can have a profound impact on the world when you allow yourself to be imperfect and still be courageous and happy. Others around you begin to take notice. Embrace your uniqueness and let your lovely, authentic self shine through!

Jenny

JENNY DOAN
MISSOURI STAR QUILT CO.

GET YOUR
DIGITAL ISSUE
TODAY!
Did you know that with every issue of BLOCK Subscription you also get a **FREE digital copy** online with exclusive bonus content in this issue! Access it in your Missouri Star account **RIGHT NOW!**

OVERCOMING CREATIVE BLOCKS

by Phillip Watts Brown

Though it can be hard to pin down an exact definition of creativity, at its core it is a kind of imaginative vitality in our thinking, a way of discovering new concepts and ideas. It can enrich our personal lives and enhance our communities. Increasingly, employers are recognizing the value of creativity in the workplace as well.

Creativity has many benefits, especially in terms of mental and emotional wellness. It stimulates multiple parts of our brains, both sharpening our thinking and leading to a state of flow. It can offer an outlet for self-expression and a way to empathize with others. It empowers and entertains us.

But if creativity is so rewarding, why is it difficult to incorporate into our lives? Why do we struggle to kindle our own creative spark or complete creative projects?

Much like difficulties with exercise, healthy eating, or other positive habits we want to practice, blocks to creativity tend to be more mental/emotional than simply a matter of finding time (though that is part of it!). If you're feeling creatively stuck, it can be helpful to explore what thoughts or beliefs might be getting in the way.

The following are five of the most common creative blocks I've observed in my work with clients as a creative coach. I'll briefly explore each one then offer a small tip for moving past them.

IMPOSTER SYNDROME

One of the biggest blocks is imposter syndrome, a sense of self-doubt or incompetence despite our experience and abilities. Thoughts like *I'm not a creative person, I'm not talented enough to do this,* or *Nobody will want what I make* stop us before we even get started.

Sometimes these are familiar criticisms from childhood echoing into our adult lives. Or they are assumptions you project onto others, trying to beat disappointment to the punch. Perhaps they are the distorted voices of depression or anxiety.

Try to identify where the thoughts originated and notice how many are actually the opinions of others. Your opinion of yourself and your creative work is the one that truly matters!

Keep that notebook or piece of paper handy whenever you're doing creative work—if self-defeating thoughts come up, simply write them down without judgment and gently return to your work. This is a process, and it will get easier with time.

If you experience depression, anxiety, or other mental health challenges, seek help from a licensed therapist who can offer additional support.

PERFECTIONISM

Perfectionism is often a response to feeling like an imposter. We think we must produce perfect work to prove our talent or our worth. *(Again, you might look to your upbringing for clues about where this thinking comes from.)*

Sometimes we feel perfection proves that creativity itself is worthy—especially of our time. And today, time is often equated with money or power. If your creativity doesn't produce sales or bring you popularity and acclaim, you worry it's frivolous or self-indulgent. Perfectionism can also be a consequence of comparison. Looking around at what everyone else is producing, you may feel like you need to be perfect to compete.

Tip

Be gentle with yourself—criticizing yourself for having these thoughts is not an effective solution! Instead, make time for some reflection or journaling to name which thoughts are coming up for you. Just getting them out of your head and onto a piece of paper can lessen their power and help you see your thoughts with more clarity.

As seen in TRIPLE PLAY BOOK

Tip

The antidote is giving yourself permission to play. That may sound childish, but think of how creative children are! You need freedom to fail, to explore, and to break out of your typical patterns.

Like a kind of stage-fright, perfectionism makes our creative muscles freeze up. Our focus narrows, our options seem limited. This is the opposite of what we need.

On a regular basis, carve out some time to create work that is just for fun. Nobody needs to see it. You don't even have to like the final product. Tell yourself that you can throw out the result—and maybe you do! Treat it as a warm-up activity or a vacation from your "serious" work.

To encourage a spirit of play, try working with new materials, especially ones that are inexpensive. Challenge yourself to make multiple versions, seeing what you learn each time. Explore a style, voice, or technique you've always admired. The possibilities are endless.

The point here is to stay open and put less pressure on the outcome. Perhaps like Google employees, who are encouraged to spend 20 percent of their time on ideas outside their regular projects, you will discover something big. Even if you don't, this practice will keep your creative muscles flexible.

THE "BLANK PAGE EFFECT"

Many writers know the paralyzing effect of staring at a completely blank page and not knowing where to begin. The same is true for all kinds of creative projects. You're facing an empty canvas or fresh block of clay. Maybe you've bought yards of beautiful fabric and are too nervous to cut it.

Tip

What is the smallest thing you can do to cross the threshold of your project? Write the words "I don't know what to write," knead the clay, or make a tiny snip in the selvage—and there, you've started. The page isn't blank anymore.

This effect can become more pronounced with larger or more detailed projects. Thinking about all the work to do, you start to feel overwhelmed. Even when you are lucky enough to have a bright, shiny idea that you're excited about, you might find yourself hesitating to take the first step or stressed trying to decide which step is, in fact, the first one.

Don't worry so much about what to do—just do something. Breathe. Move your body. Rub your palms together and feel that heat. There is energy in action, no matter how small. Let it carry you to the next smallest thing you can do.

Also keep in mind that the creative process is messy and usually involves several revisions or restarts. Lower the stakes by reminding yourself that you probably can (and will) make changes once you get going.

NOT FEELING INSPIRED

Inspiration—that sudden spark, that urge to create—is a great motivator. However, it doesn't strike all the time. There are days (or weeks or months) when we don't feel very inspired.

Inspiration is not a requirement for engaging in creative work. In fact, it's often the reverse: working invites inspiration. Maya Angelou once said, "When I'm writing, I write. And then it's as if the muse is convinced that I'm serious and says 'Okay. Okay. I'll come.'"

Tip

Author Elizabeth Gilbert's suggests you follow your curiosity rather than your passion. Passion is a lot to live up to! Curiosity, on the other hand, offers a more approachable entry point. If you're not feeling very curious, take a walk or read a book or play around with your materials and see what sparks an interest, big or small.

Whether or not we have a regular creative practice, this principle is still true—we are far more likely to find inspiration when we actively engage our creativity than when we wait for the muse to find us. So, how do you start if you're not feeling it?

Then, follow that curiosity where it leads you. Research, write, experiment, ask more questions. And if something else crosses your path that seems more interesting, allow yourself to follow that. (Gilbert compares the movement to a hummingbird flitting from flower to flower.) This process is, in itself, an exercise in creative thinking. Don't be surprised if you find a little inspiration along the way.

FINDING THE TIME

Lastly, we tackle the most practical obstacle to creativity: busyness. Though this is usually the first problem we focus on, it often resolves itself when we handle the previous four concerns. We find the time because we aren't so caught in avoidance.

However, it's true that many of us are busy people, juggling work, family, and relationships, and it can seem hard to find time for creative work. That said, some faulty assumptions might be getting in the way, like "I don't have any spare time," or "Creative work requires a lot of time."

Tip

Just like exercise, a little creativity on a regular basis is better than no creativity at all. Instead of waiting for a large chunk of time, maximize moments of time. A few minutes first thing in the morning or before you go to bed, maybe as an afternoon break. Those small moments add up to quite a significant effort in the long run.

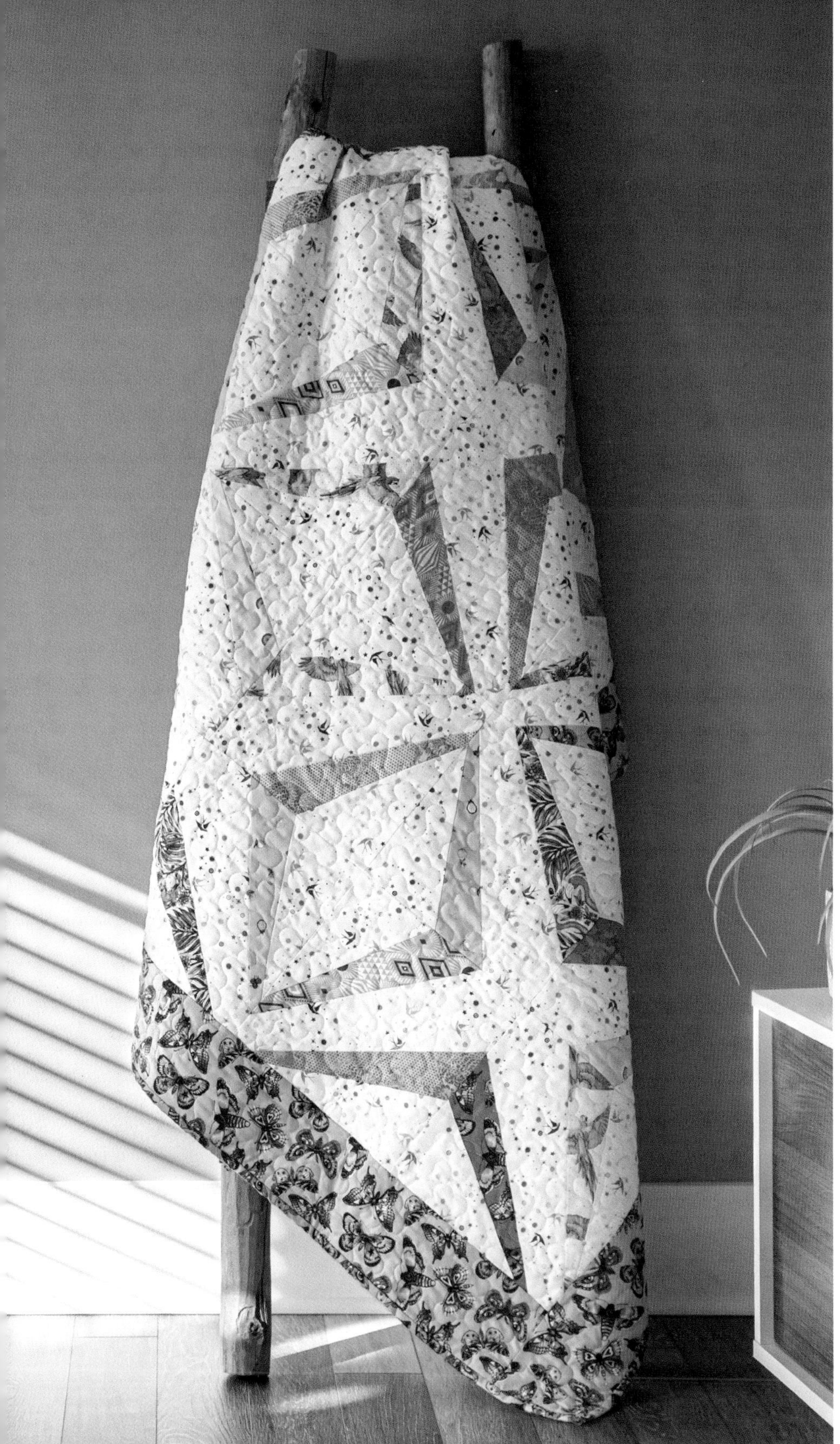

There may be more spare moments in your day than you think, especially spent scrolling through your phone or watching tv. While neither of those is necessarily bad, they often steal more of our time than we realize, making them a perfect place to recover a few spare minutes.

One idea is to set a timer for 10 minutes (even 5 minutes will do) and then focus on your creative work until the timer goes off. You will be amazed how long 10 uninterrupted minutes can feel. If you have more time, you can work for a longer period. Honor this time by minimizing distractions. Most things can wait 10 minutes.

If your creative work can stay laid out or easily accessible, it makes it easy to squeeze in a few minutes here and there whenever you can. Or, if you prefer a more orderly approach, schedule a specific time for creativity on a regular basis.

This is not an exhaustive list, and there are a multitude of ways that you can move beyond your blocks to connect with your creativity! Try out different methods and see what works for you. Trust your intuition. I believe human beings are inherently creative—and that, with small moves like the ones in this list, we can reconnect with the vibrance of our own creative potential.

Print Out Your Own Creative Affirmations
msqc.co/affirmation-cards

Boardwalk

Do you enjoy long, romantic walks to the sewing room? This lovely Boardwalk quilt is the perfect scrappy project to get you in a sewing mood. Created with a mix of fun prints for an eclectic look, this quilt is reminiscent of the wooden planks we promenade on by the shore. It's an easy, breezy project that's practically a vacation!

MATERIALS

QUILT SIZE
70½" x 94½"

BLOCK SIZES

- A - 5" x 16" unfinished, 4½" x 15½" finished
- B - 5" x 7½" unfinished, 4½" x 7" finished
- C - 5" x 7½" unfinished, 4½" x 7" finished
- D - 5" x 10" unfinished, 4½" x 9½" finished
- E - 5" x 24½" unfinished, 4½" x 24" finished
- F - 5" x 12" unfinished, 4½" x 11½" finished

QUILT TOP
1 package of 10" print squares
1½ yards of coordinating print fabric
- includes outer border
¼ yard each of 3 different print fabrics
1 roll of 1½" background strips
- includes sashing and inner border

BINDING
¾ yard

BACKING
5¾ yards - vertical seam(s)
or 3 yards of 108" wide

SAMPLE QUILT
Kasuri Artisan Batiks & **Artisan Batiks Magical Winter** by Lunn Studios for Robert Kaufman

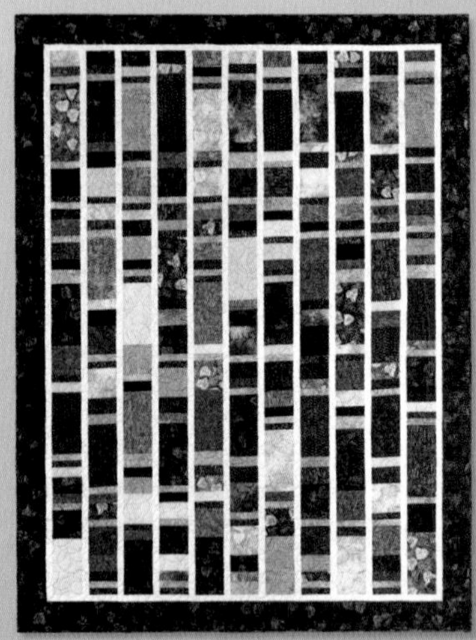

1 cut

From the coordinating print fabric, cut (1) 10″ strip across the width of the fabric. Subcut (4) 10″ squares and add these to your package of print squares. Set the remaining fabric aside for the outer border.

Cut each 10″ print square in half to yield a **total of (92)** 5″ x 10″ rectangles.

- Subcut (38) 5″ x 10″ rectangles into (1) 5″ square, (1) 5″ x 3″ rectangle, and (1) 5″ x 2″ rectangle.

- Subcut (11) 5″ x 10″ rectangles into (2) 5″ x 3″ rectangles, and (2) 5″ x 2″ rectangles. Set (1) 5″ x 3″ rectangle aside for another project.

- Subcut (3) 5″ x 10″ rectangles into (5) 5″ x 2″ rectangles.

- Subcut (1) 5″ x 10″ rectangle into (2) 5″ x 2″ rectangles. Set (1) 5″ x 6″ rectangle aside for another project.

You will have a **total of (39)** 5″ x 10″ rectangles, a **total of (38)** 5″ squares, a **total of (59)** 5″ x 3″ rectangles, and a **total of (77)** 5″ x 2″ rectangles.

From each of the print fabrics, cut (5) 1½″ strips across the width of the fabric. Subcut the strips into a **total of (117)** 1½″ x 5″ rectangles. Set the remaining fabric aside for another project.

2 block construction

Block A

Arrange (1) 5″ x 3″ print rectangle, (1) 5″ x 2″ print rectangle, (2) 5″ x 1½″ print rectangles, and (1) 5″ x 10″ print rectangle in a column as shown. Sew the units together and press. **Make 18**. **2A**

Block A Size: 5″ x 16″ unfinished, 4½″ x 15½″ finished

Block B

Arrange (1) 5″ x 2″ print rectangle, (1) 5″ x 1½″ print rectangle, and (1) 5″ print square in a column as shown. Sew the units together and press. **Make 18**. **2B**

Block B Size: 5″ x 7½″ unfinished, 4½″ x 7″ finished

Block C

Arrange (2) 5″ x 1½″ print rectangles, (1) 5″ x 2″ print rectangle, (1) 5″ x 3″ print rectangle, and (1) 5″ x 1½″ print rectangle in a column as shown. Sew the units together and press. **Make 6**. **2C**

Block C Size: 5″ x 7½″ unfinished, 4½″ x 7″ finished

2A

2B

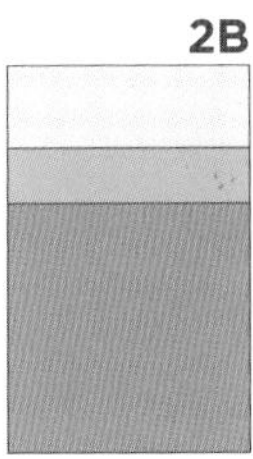

2C

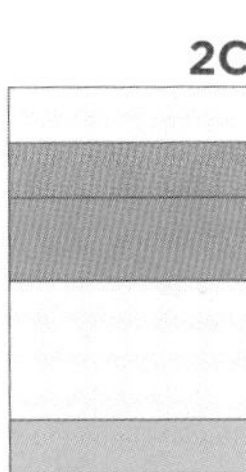

1 Arrange (1) 5″ x 3″ print rectangle, (1) 5″ x 2″ print rectangle, (2) 5″ x 1½″ print rectangles, and (1) 5″ x 10″ print rectangle in a column as shown. Sew the units together and press. Make 18.

2 Arrange (1) 5″ x 2″ print rectangle, (1) 5″ x 1½″ print rectangle, and (1) 5″ print square in a column as shown. Sew the units together and press. Make 18.

3 Arrange (2) 5″ x 1½″ print rectangles, (1) 5″ x 2″ print rectangle, (1) 5″ x 3″ print rectangle, and (1) 5″ x 1½″ print rectangle in a column as shown. Sew the units together and press. Make 6.

4 No sewing is needed to create Block D. Use a total of (6) 5″ x 10″ print rectangles for Block D.

5 Arrange (1) 5″ x 1½″ print rectangle, (1) 5″ print square, (1) 5″ x 3″ print rectangle, (1) 5″ x 2″ print rectangle, (1) 5″ x 10″ print rectangle, (1) 5″ x 1½″ print rectangle, (1) 5″ x 2″ print rectangle, and (1) 5″ x 3″ print rectangle in a column as shown. Sew the units together and press. Make 15.

6 Arrange (1) 5″ x 1½″ print rectangle, (1) 5″ print square, (1) 5″ x 3″ print rectangle, (1) 5″ x 2″ print rectangle, and (2) 5″ x 1½″ print rectangles in a column as shown. Sew the units together and press. Make 5.

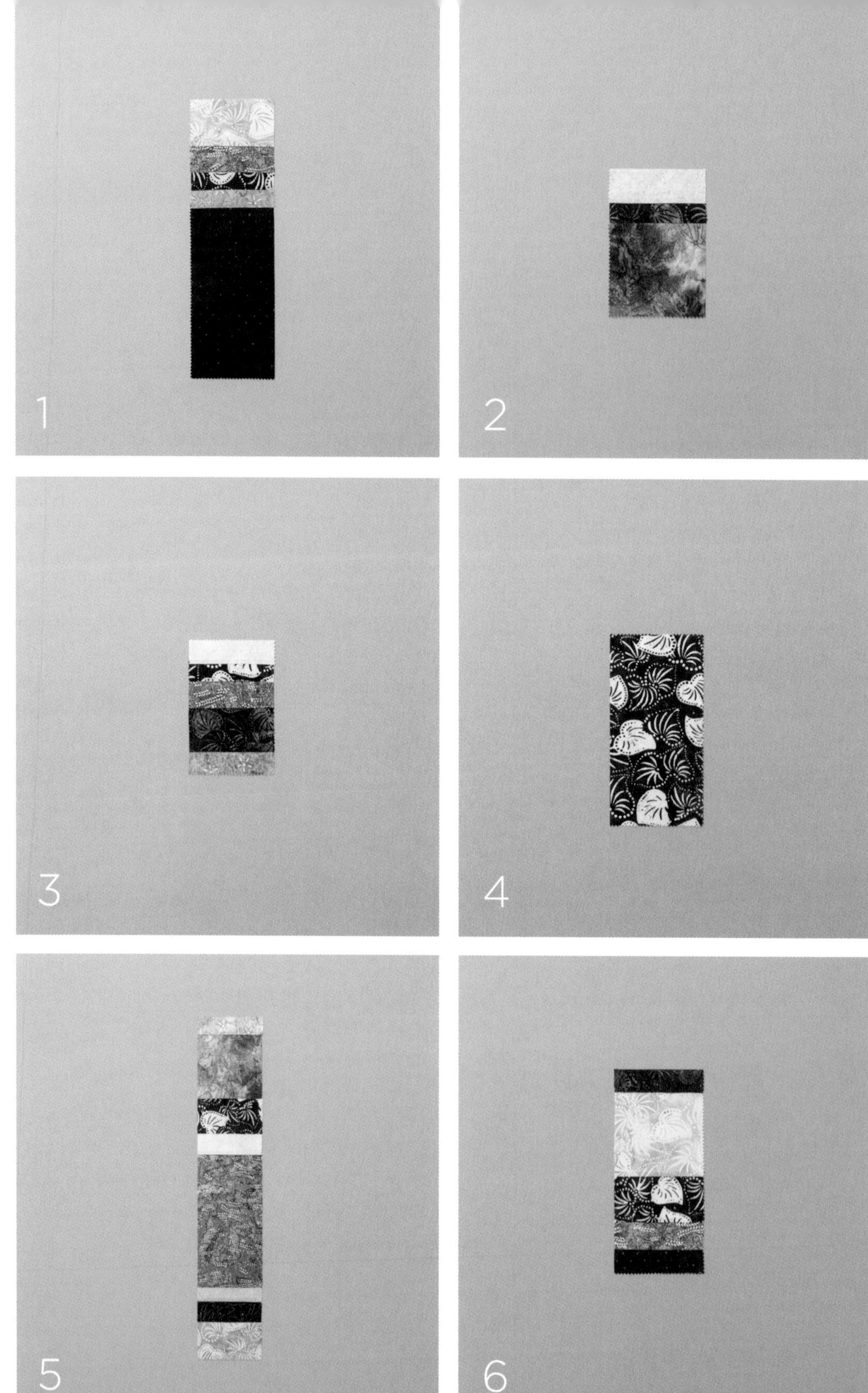

Block D

No sewing is needed to create Block D. Use a **total of (6)** 5″ x 10″ print rectangles for Block D. **2D**

Block D Size: 5″ x 10″ unfinished, 4½″ x 9½″ finished

Block E

Arrange (1) 5″ x 1½″ print rectangle, (1) 5″ print square, (1) 5″ x 3″ print rectangle, (1) 5″ x 2″ print rectangle, (1) 5″ x 10″ print rectangle, (1) 5″ x 1½″ print rectangle, (1) 5″ x 2″ print rectangle, and (1) 5″ x 3″ print rectangle in a column as shown. Sew the units together and press. **Make 15**. **2E**

Block E Size: 5″ x 24½″ unfinished, 4½″ x 24″ finished

Block F

Arrange (1) 5″ x 1½″ print rectangle, (1) 5″ print square, (1) 5″ x 3″ print rectangle, (1) 5″ x 2″ print rectangle, and (2) 5″ x 1½″ print rectangles in a column as shown. Sew the units together and press. **Make 5**. **2F**

Block F Size: 5″ x 12″ unfinished, 4½″ x 11½″ finished

3 make columns

Column 1

Arrange 8 blocks in A, B, C, A, B, A, B, D order from top to bottom. **Note**: Some of our blocks are rotated 180° for more variety. Sew the units together and press. **Make 6**. **3A**

Column 2

Arrange 4 blocks in E, E, E, F order from top to bottom. Sew the units together and press. **Make 5**. **3B**

Measure the length of each column. Each column 1 should be ½" longer than each column 2. Trim each column 1 to the length of column 2, approximately 84". You can trim from the top or bottom to add more variety to the horizontal patterns in the quilt top.

4 sashing

From the roll of 1½" background strips, sew 27 strips together to make 1 long strip. Trim 10 sashing strips from this long strip to the length of your rows, approximately 84". Set the remainder of the long strip aside for the inner border.

5 arrange & sew

Arrange the columns as shown in diagram **5A** on page 21, alternating between columns 1 and 2. Sew the columns together with a sashing strip in between each column. Press.

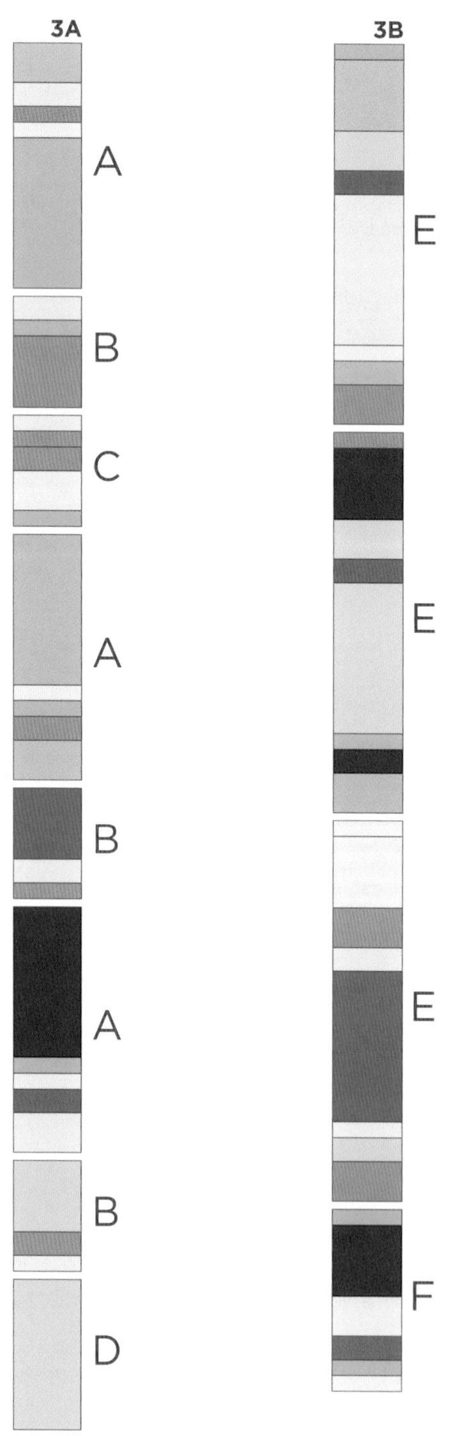

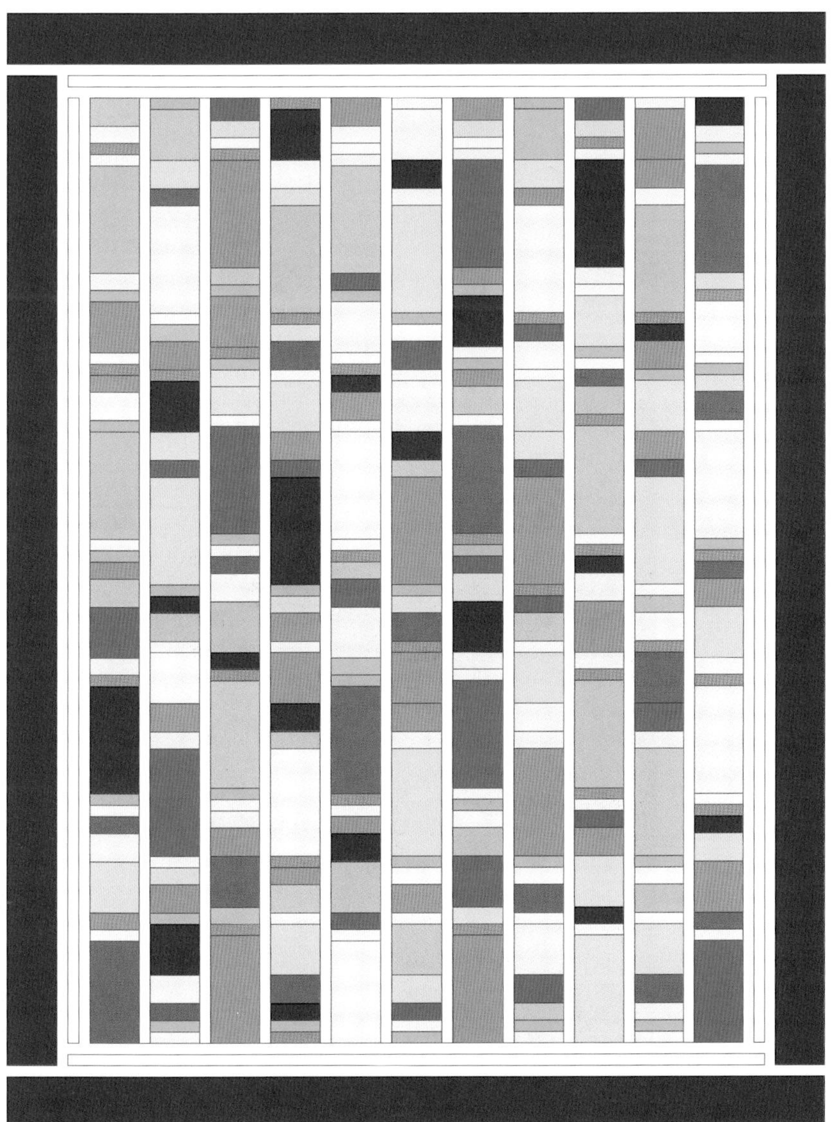

6 inner border

Trim the borders from the 1½″ background strip set aside previously. Refer to Borders (pg. 118) in the Construction Basics to measure, cut, and attach the borders. The strip lengths are approximately 84″ for the sides and 62″ for the top and bottom.

7 outer border

Cut (8) 5″ strips across the width of the outer border fabric. Sew the strips together to make 1 long strip. Trim the borders from this strip. Refer to Borders (pg. 118) in the Construction Basics to measure, cut, and attach the borders. The lengths are approximately 86″ for the sides and 71″ for the top and bottom.

8 quilt & bind

Layer the quilt with batting and backing, then quilt. After the quilting is complete, see Construction Basics (pg. 118) to add binding and finish your quilt.

Layered Diamonds

What's even better than diamonds? Layers and layers of them! Add extra sparkle to this lovely quilt design with tiny secondary diamonds right at the points of larger diamonds. Made with our Large Missouri Star Simple Wedge Template with its accompanying Wing Template, It's a stunning quilt that's a snap to make!

WRITE THE STORY

MATERIALS

QUILT SIZE
63″ x 60½″

BLOCK SIZE
8½″ x 7″ unfinished, 8″ x 6½″ finished

QUILT TOP
1 package of 10″ print squares
¼ yard each of 2 different accent fabrics

INNER BORDER
½ yard

OUTER BORDER
1¼ yards

BINDING
¾ yard

BACKING
4 yards – vertical seam(s)
or 2 yards of 108″ wide

OTHER
Missouri Star Quilt Co.
Large Wing Template
Missouri Star Large Simple Wedge
Template for 10″ Squares

SAMPLE QUILT
Blue Breeze by Danhui Nai
for Wilmington Prints

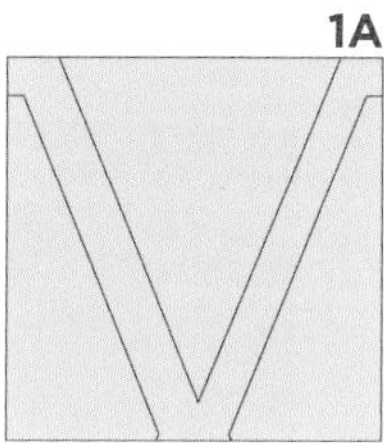

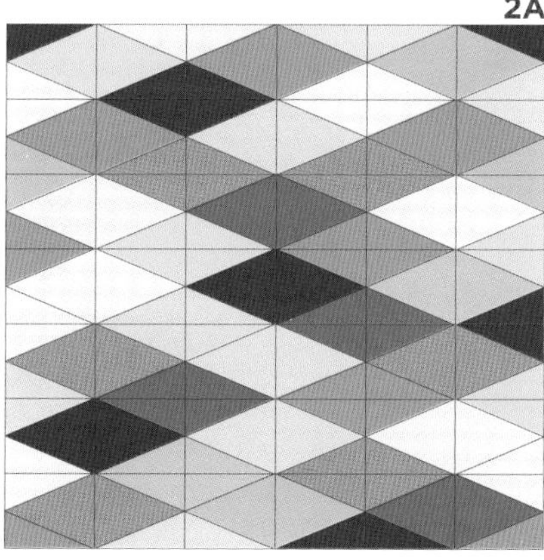

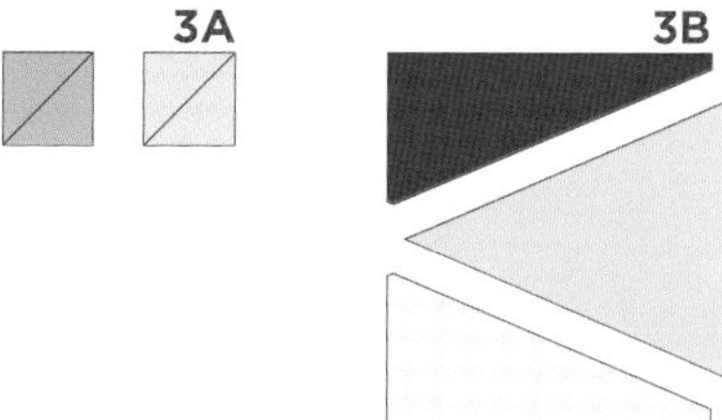

1 cut

Note: You will need 21 pairs of matching 10″ print squares if you would like to have the same effect as our quilt.

From each 10″ print square, cut 1 wedge and 2 wings—1 wing will be reversed. **1A**

From each accent fabric, cut (3) 2½″ strips across the width of the fabric. Subcut a **total of (48)** 2½″ squares of each fabric.

2 arrange

It is best to lay this quilt out before sewing any pieces together. Lay out the wedges and wings to form the quilt center as shown. Notice how 2 matching wedges or 4 matching wings come together to form a diamond shape. **2A**

3 block construction

Tip: To stay well organized, only remove the pieces from your layout that you will be sewing and then put them back before moving on to the next block.

Mark a diagonal line on the reverse side of each 2½″ accent square. Set the squares aside for now. **3A**

Begin in the top corner and pick up the first 3 pieces in the first column—1 wedge and 2 wings. **3B**

1. Select 1 wedge and 2 wings that are each cut from a different fabric. Arrange them as shown.

2. Flip the wedge over on top of the upper wing so they are right sides together. Align the slanted edges, then sew along the slanted edge.

3. Open and press the seam allowance towards the wing.

4. Place the remaining wing on top of the other slanted edge of the wedge with right sides together. Sew along the slanted edge.

5. Open and press. Measure ¼″ past the sewn intersection at the tip of the wedge and trim the block. Measure 8½″ away and trim it again. Measure 3½″ vertically from the sewn intersection and trim again to yield a 8½″ x 7″ block.

6. Place a marked 2½″ accent square on the 2 corners of the block with right sides facing and the marked line of each square crossing over the seams below. Sew on the marked lines, then trim the excess fabric. Press. Make 42.

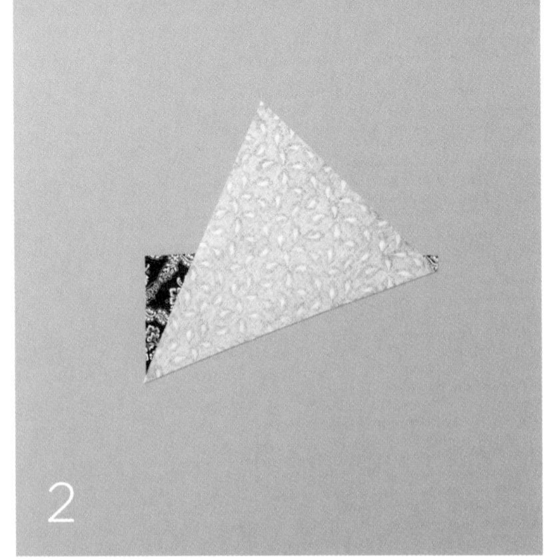

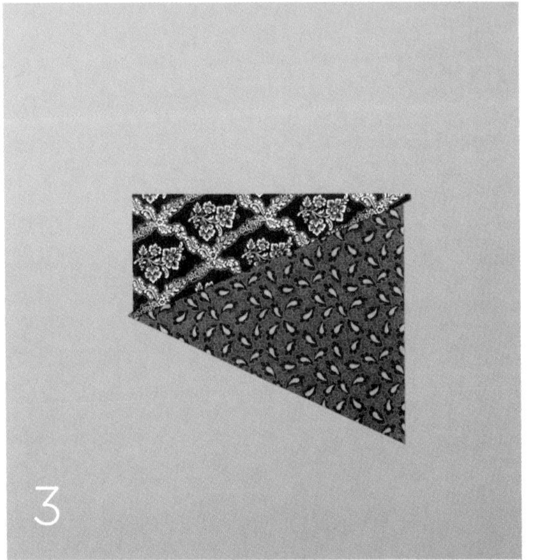

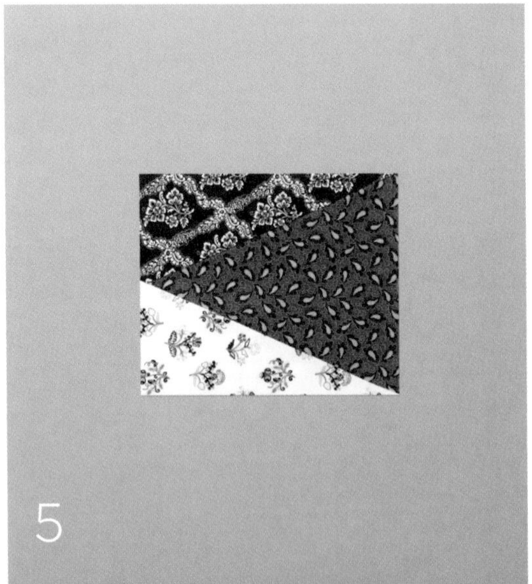

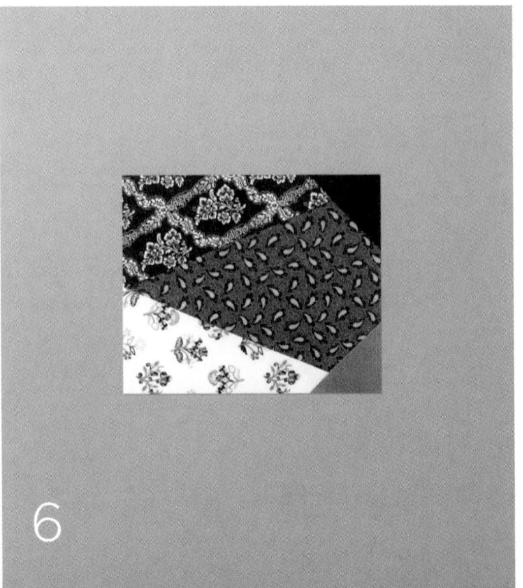

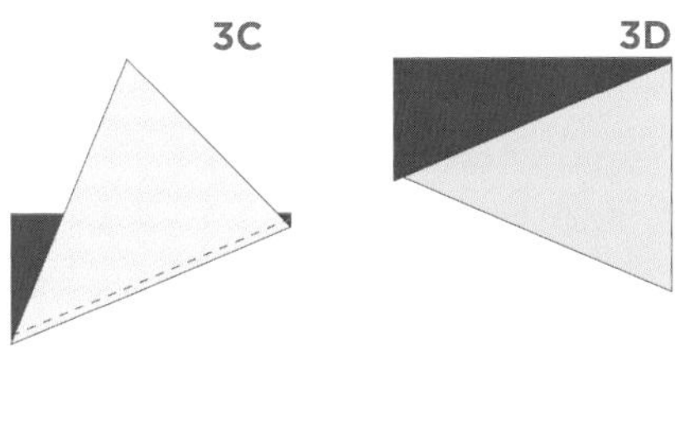

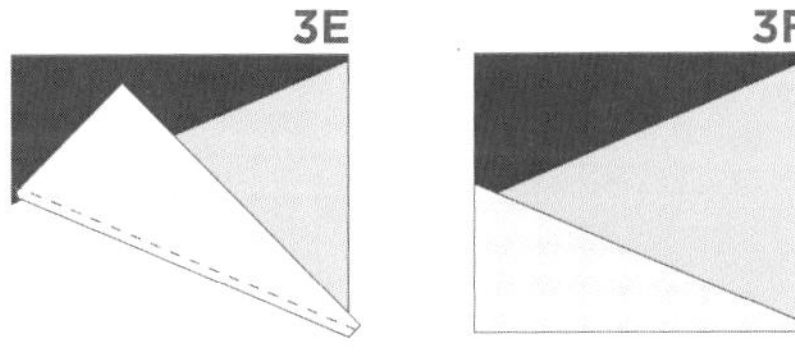

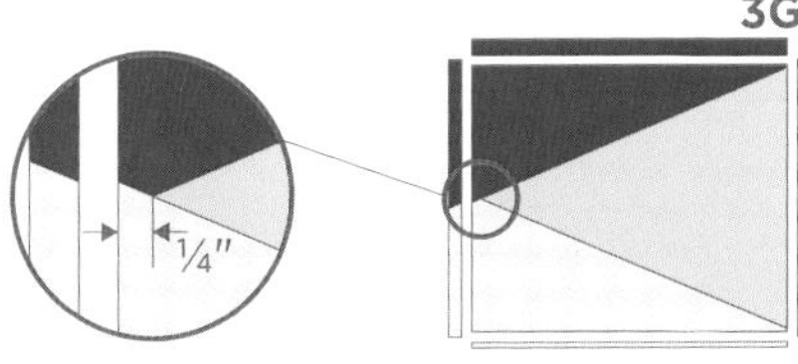

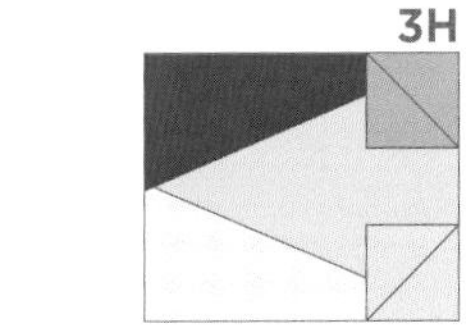

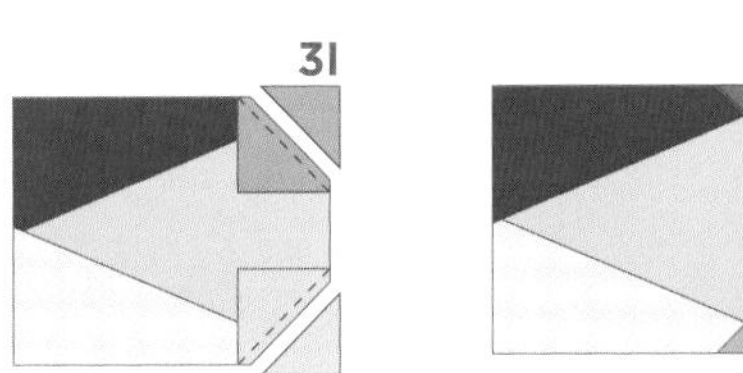

Place the wedge on top of 1 wing, right sides facing. Be careful not to stretch the fabric and sew along the slanted edge as shown. Press. **3C 3D**

Place the other wing on top of the unit, right sides facing, and carefully sew along the slanted edge as shown. Press. **3E 3F**

Leave ¼″ past the point of the wedge and trim the unit to 8½″ x 7″. **3G**

Pick up 1 of each accent square and lay them right sides facing on top of the unit, as shown. **Note**: As you create the blocks, make sure you are placing the same accent fabric on the same corner of each block. **3H**

Sew on the marked lines, then trim the excess fabric ¼″ away from the sewn seam. Press. **Make 42** blocks. Set the remaining accent squares aside for the inner border. **3I 3J**

Block Size: 8½″ x 7″ unfinished,
8″ x 6½″ finished

4 sew the quilt center

Once all of the blocks are completed, sew them together in rows. Each row will be made up of **6 blocks** and there are **7 rows**. Press the rows in opposite directions. Nest the seams and sew the rows together. Press.

5 inner border

Note: The top and bottom borders on this quilt are sewn on first and the sides are sewn on second.

From the inner border fabric, cut (5) 2½" strips across the fabric. From 3 of the strips, subcut a **total of (12)** 2½" x 8½" rectangles. Set the ends of the trimmed strip and the 2 full strips aside for a moment.

Note: The order in which you place the accent squares in the borders is important and you may find it helpful to consult the diagram on page 29 before sewing.

Lay 6 of the 2½" x 8½" rectangles you just made in a row. Place the accent squares you set aside earlier on the ends of the rectangles as shown with right sides facing. **5A**

Sew on the marked lines, then trim the excess fabric ¼" away from the sewn seam. Press. Sew the rectangles together to make a row. **Make 2** rows for the top and bottom inner borders. The rows should each measure approximately 48½". **5B 5C**

Refer to Borders (pg. 118) in the Construction Basics to measure, cut, and attach the top and bottom borders.

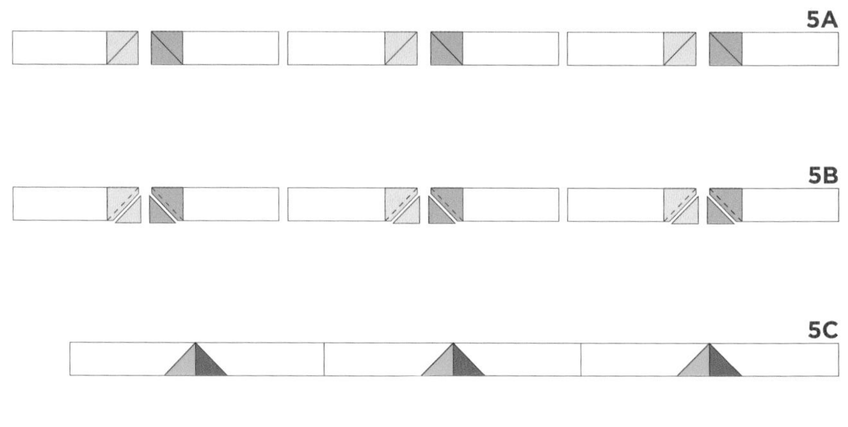

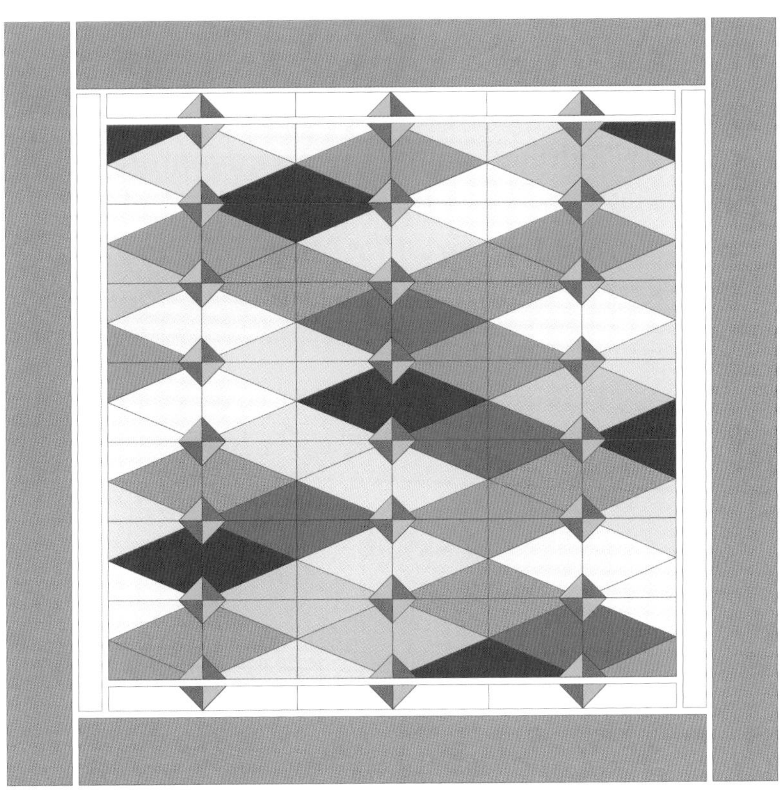

Pick up the full and partial strips you set aside earlier and sew them together to form 1 long strip. Trim the side borders from these strips. Refer to Borders (pg. 118) in the Construction Basics to measure, cut, and attach the side borders. They should measure approximately 50″.

6 outer border

From the outer border fabric, cut (6) 6″ strips across the width of the fabric. Sew the strips together to make 1 long strip. Trim the borders from this strip. Refer to Borders (pg. 118) in the Construction Basics to measure, cut, and attach the borders. The lengths are approximately 52½″ for the top and bottom and 61″ for the sides.

7 quilt & bind

Layer the quilt with batting and backing, then quilt. After the quilting is complete, see Construction Basics (pg. 118) to add binding and finish your quilt.

THE QUILTING **MARINE**

"Quilting is an amazing adventure. It's the best therapy. I fell in love from the very first stitch."
-Mark Darrell, the Quilting Marine

Mark Darrell is a twenty-year Marine Corps veteran who has long suffered the debilitating effects of PTSD. In 2016, he stepped into the quilting world. Right away, he noticed the peace and healing that quilt making can bring.

In just a few short years, Mark has built an incredible online community where he shares his expertise and his journey. He is known as the Quilting Marine, and he proves what we have always known: Quilting has the power to change lives.

Mark's signature technique is crumb piecing. He starts with piles of random scraps, then he sews and chops (and sews and chops) until, bit by bit, all those tiny pieces form a dazzlingly intricate block. For Mark, that process of creating order from chaos soothes the pain of PTSD.

Last summer, Mark joined one of our Missouri Star LIVE tutorials to demonstrate how to make his Crumb Quilting Stars pattern. We all fell in love with his story and his talent for teaching. Now, we are delighted to share his newest pattern, Emotion Shadow Block.

We had the opportunity to chat with Mark and learn a bit more about this incredible man:

Tell us about yourself. Where did you grow up? What led you to join the Marines?
I grew up in Bay Shore, New York. I joined the Marine Corps delayed entry program after the Beirut barracks bombing that killed 220 Marines. I walked into a Marine Corps recruiting station and wanted nothing but the infantry. I went to MCRD (Marine Corps Recruit Depot) Parris Island, South Carolina, in July of 1986.

How has quilting helped you during challenging times?
Piecing helps to steady my mind. It keeps me in the present moment. When I'm in crisis from PTSD, I go to my quilt room to work on a current project. In extreme cases, I crumb piece to quiet my thoughts.

You call crumb-pieced blocks "Emotion Blocks." What do they mean to you?
My Emotion Blocks represent the confusion, aimlessness, and violence of my own trauma. When I add them to a quilt, it feels like I'm letting go of some of the pain. The repetitiveness of building a block keeps me sane. Even though the process is repeated, the result is different every time.

What led you to start quilting? Tell us about the very first quilt you ever made.
When my first grandson, Jax, was born, I felt the urge to create something for him that was unique—something that could not be purchased. I thought, "Why not a quilt?" So with no prior experience or training, I started the journey of learning to quilt. I began by watching Missouri Star tutorials, and what a great choice that was. The rest is history. Jenny means the world to me and my path in quilting.

Talk about your quilting process. What inspires you to make a new quilt design?
I like to watch other quilters and add or take away from what they have created to make it my own. I have recently found Bruce Seeds and his amazing kaleidoscope mosaics. They have me mesmerized, and this is my next path; the one-block wonders.

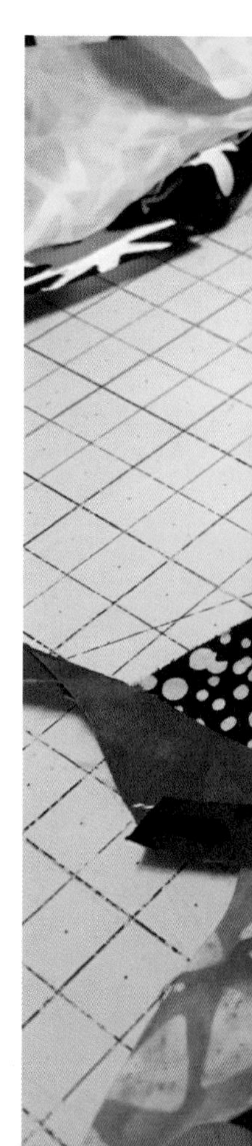

What has been your favorite quilt design?

The New York Beauty is my absolute favorite of all time ... so far. I gave my first New York Beauty to my mother-in-law for her birthday. I rarely keep quilts. I love to piece the blocks together, and I love to give quilts away for someone else to enjoy. It's the building of the quilts that is my therapy; the finished product isn't as satisfying to me as the path to the completed quilt. And I never quilt for money. If I were to charge for one of my builds, I would risk losing what quilting means to me.

What have you learned from your mistakes?

I'm still learning from mistakes. And, I love to make them. If I make a mistake, I can save someone else from making that same mistake. Quilts are forgiving and quilters are the most giving people in the world. I love to see the expressions people have when I give them a quilt; it's very satisfying.

Talk about the quilt design you created for this issue of BLOCK. What inspired you to make it?

The Emotion Shadow Block Quilt was designed for my amazing wife Yvonne. It is a small symbol to thank her for what she means to me. She has loved and supported me through my darkest hours. Without her, I would not be here to teach others.

What have you learned about quilting since you began?

Don't let this craft cause you stress. No one's life ever depended on a perfect quarter-inch seam allowance. There are way more important things in life. It's only fabric and its only thread. That's my mantra.

Learn more by following The Quilting Marine:
youtube.com/thequiltingmarine
facebook.com/thequiltingmarine
instagram.com/thequiltingmarine

MATERIALS

QUILT SIZE
53″ x 58½″

BLOCK SIZE
7″ x 12″ unfinished, 6½″ x 11½″ finished

QUILT TOP
1 roll of 2½″ print strips*
¾ yard of accent fabric
1 yard of background fabric
- includes inner border

BINDING
½ yard

BACKING
3½ yards - horizontal seam(s)

**Scraps can be used to make crumb-pieced slabs if you prefer.*

SAMPLE QUILT
Sunkist Soleil and **Naturally Neutral Batik Solids - Cream** by Kathy Engle for Island Batik
Artisan Batiks Solids - Prisma Dyes Black by Lunn Studios for Robert Kaufman

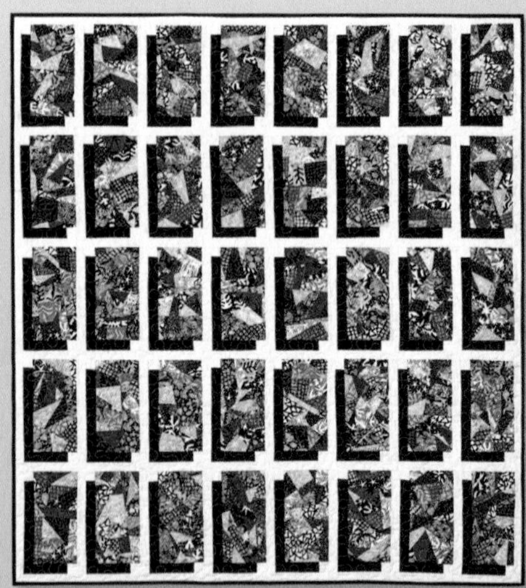

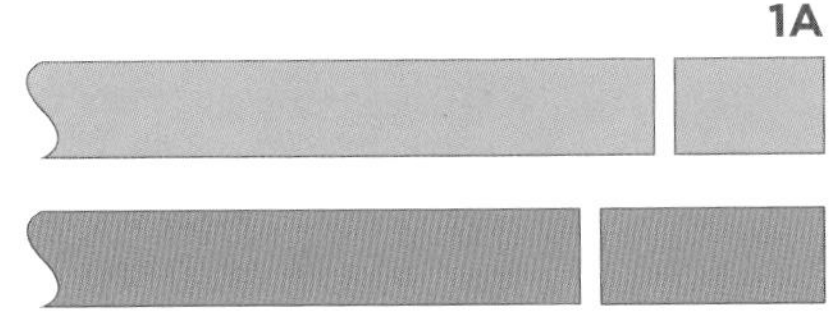

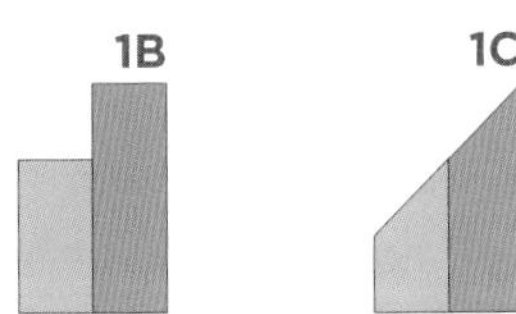

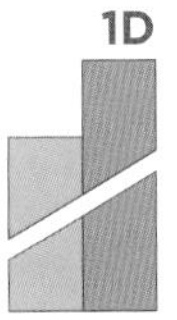

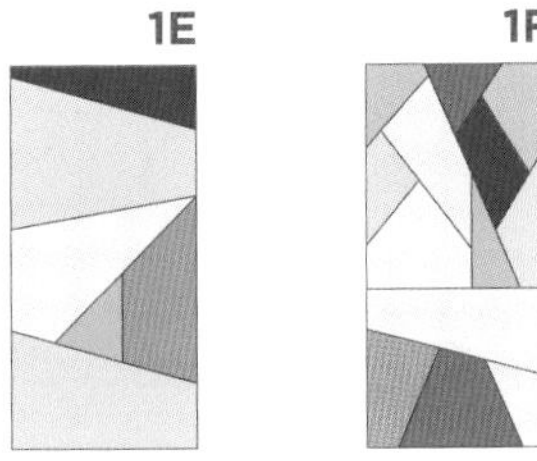

1 make the crumb blocks

Note: This is a very improvisational process. Exact dimensions for making crumb slabs will not be given. How you choose to sew your pieces together is entirely up to you entirely. Our slabs were made using 2½" strips, but you can use squares or scraps instead.

Start with (2) 2½" strips from your roll. Cut a segment from each strip that is about 4-6" long. **1A**

Sew the 2 segments together, then press. **1B**

Trim your unit as you wish. Some options for trimming are:

- Trim your unit at an angle. **1C**
- Cut your unit into smaller pieces. These smaller pieces can be sewn together to make new slabs! **1D**

Continue cutting and attaching segments of your desired length from your 2½" strips to your slab. Remember to trim your slab after attaching each new segment. **1E**

Tip: You can make smaller slabs and sew them together to form larger slabs. **1F**

When your slab has reached at least 5" x 10", trim it square.

Slab Size: 5" x 10" unfinished, 4½" x 9½" finished

Make 40 slabs.

2 cut

From the accent fabric, cut (15) 1½" strips across the width of the fabric.

- From 10 of the strips, subcut a **total of (40)** 1½" x 9" rectangles.
- From 5 of the strips, subcut a **total of (40)** 1½" x 5" rectangles.

From the background fabric,cut (17) 1½" strips across the width of the fabric.

- From each of 8 of the strips, subcut (3) 1½" x 11" rectangles and (1) 1½" x 7" rectangle.
- From 6 strips, subcut 16 additional 1½" x 11" rectangles for a **total of 40**.
- Set 3 strips aside for the border.

3 sew the units

Sew a 1½" background square to 1 end of each 1½" x 9" accent rectangle. Press. We'll call these long units for clarity. **3A**

Sew a 1½" background square to 1 end of each 1½" x 5" accent rectangle. Press. We'll call these short units for clarity. **3B**

4 block construction

Sew a long unit to the left side of each crumb-pieced slab as shown. Press. **4A**

Sew a short unit to the bottom of each crumb-pieced slab as shown. Press. **4B**

1. Sew a 1½″ square to 1 end of each 1½″ x 5″ rectangle. Press.
2. Sew a 1½″ square to 1 end of each 1½″ x 9″ rectangle. Press.
3. Sew a 1½″ x 10″ pieced rectangle to the left side of each crumb pieced rectangle. Press.
4. Sew a 1½″ x 6″ pieced rectangle to the bottom of each unit. Press.
5. Sew a 1½″ x 11″ background rectangle to the left side of each unit. Press.
6. Sew a 1½″ x 7″ background rectangle to the bottom of each unit. Press.

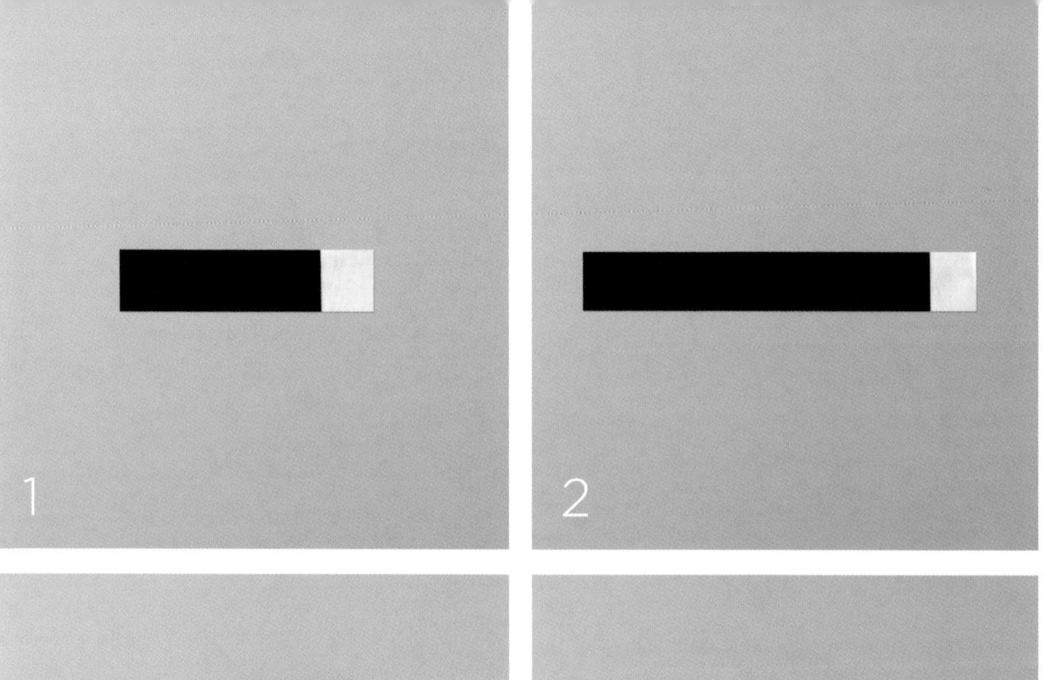

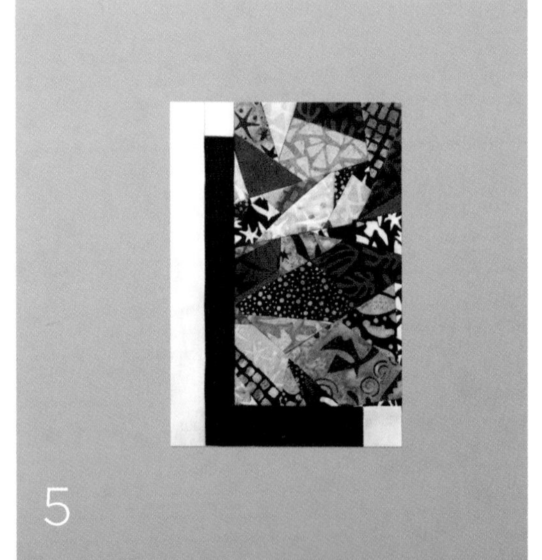

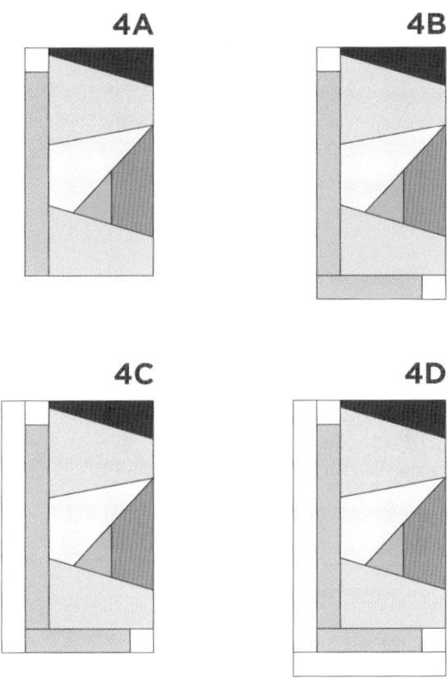

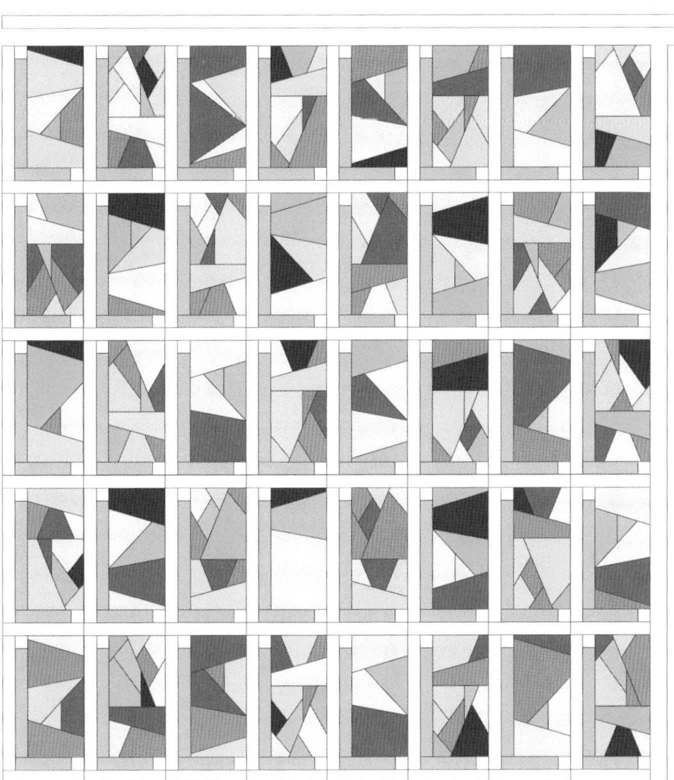

Sew a 1½" x 11" background rectangle to the left edge of the unit. Press. **4C**

Sew a 1½" x 7" background rectangle to the bottom and press to complete the block. **Make 40**. **4D**

Block Size: 7" x 12" unfinished, 6½" x 11½" finished

5 arrange & sew

Refer to diagram **5A** to arrange your blocks in **5 rows of 8**. Sew the blocks together to form rows. Press the seams of each row in opposite directions. Nest the seams and sew the rows together. Press.

6 border

Note: The border is only sewn onto the right and top sides of the quilt.

Sew the (3) 1½" background strips you set aside earlier together to form a long strip. Cut the borders from this strip. Refer to Borders (pg. 118) in the Construction Basics to measure, cut, and attach the borders. The strip lengths are approximately 58" for the right side and 53½" for the top.

7 quilt & bind

Layer the quilt with batting and backing, then quilt. See Construction Basics (pg. 118) to add binding and finish your quilt.

STACCATO STAR

SEW-ALONG *PART ONE*

QUILT SIZE
97" x 97"

MORNING GLORY BLOCK SIZE
16½" unfinished, 16" finished

STUDIO STAR BLOCK SIZE
10½" unfinished, 10" finished

ENTIRE QUILT TOP
3 packages of Staccato Star 10" squares*
¼ yard of fabric D**

INNER BORDER
¾ yard**

OUTER BORDER
2 yards**

BINDING
1 yard**

BACKING
8¾ yards - vertical seam(s) or 3 yards of 108" wide

RECOMMENDED
Missouri Star Drunkard's Path Circle Template Set - Small
Clearly Perfect Slotted Trimmer B or Bloc Loc 4½" Square Up Ruler

4 packages of 10" print squares can be substituted for the package of Staccato Star squares. You will need a **total of (148) 10" squares.*

Other packages of squares may not have the same number of duplicate prints needed to match the quilt exactly.

***The ¼ yard of fabric D, ¾ yard for the inner border, 2 yards for the outer border, and 1 yard binding are included in the Staccato Star kit.*

BLOCK SUPPLIES - MORNING GLORY
(2) 10" fabric A squares
(1) 10" fabric B square
(1) 10" fabric C square
(1) 10" fabric D square
(1) 10" fabric F square
(1) 10" fabric H square
(2) 2½" fabric D strips

***Note**: Fabrics E, G, and I-N are not used in this block.*

BLOCK SUPPLIES - STUDIO STAR
(2) 10" fabric A squares
(3) 10" fabric B squares
(4) 10" fabric F squares
(4) 10" fabric G squares
(2) 10" fabric J squares
(3) 10" fabric L squares

***Notes**:*
- *Fabrics C, D, E, H, I, K, M, and N are not used in these blocks.*
- *We will be making dark and light versions of the Studio Star. We have kept the directions for each version separate to minimize confusion.*

TOTAL FABRIC REQUIRED IF YOU ARE SELECTING YOUR OWN:
Fabric A - ¾ yard
Fabric B - ¾ yard
Fabric C - ½ yard
Fabric D - ½ yard
Fabric E - 1 yard
Fabric F - 1¾ yards
Fabric G - 1¾ yards
Fabric H - 1 yard
Fabric I - 1 yard
Fabric J - 1 yard
Fabric K - ¾ yard
Fabric L - 2 yards
Fabric M - 1 yard
Fabric N - 1 yard

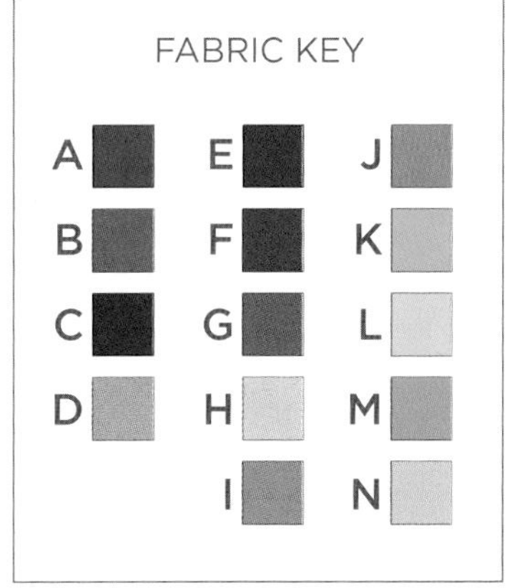

PRINT OUT YOUR OWN FABRIC KEY
msqc.co/staccato-star-fabric-key

MORNING GLORY

1 cut

Tip: You can save any partial squares you have for increased variety in Part 5.

- From (1) 10″ fabric A square, cut (1) 2½″ strip across the width of the square.
    - Subcut the strip into (4) 2½″ squares. Set the remaining portion aside.

Gather the remaining fabric A square and the squares of fabrics B, C, F, and H.

- Cut each square in half vertically and horizontally to create 5″ squares.
    - Trim (2) 5″ squares of both fabrics B and C to 4½″.
    - Set (2) 5″ squares each of F and H aside.

- From (1) 10″ fabric D square, cut (2) 4½″ strips across the squares.
    - Subcut a **total of (4)** 4½″ squares.

- From the (2) 2½″ fabric D strips, cut a **total of (4)** 2½″ x 16½″ border rectangles.

Place (1) 5″ fabric F square on your cutting surface. Lay template A on top of your square with the 4½″ marks at the top and left edges of the square. Carefully cut around the curve. Trim and discard the small ends of the corner piece. **1A**

Turn the quarter-circle piece 180°. Lay template A on top of your quarter-circle with the 4½″ marks at the top and left edges. Carefully cut around the curve to create another corner piece. Repeat to **make 4** corner pieces each of fabrics F and H. **1B 1C**

Gather the (4) 5″ fabric A squares, (2) 5″ fabric B squares, and (2) 5″ fabric C squares. Lay a fabric A square on your cutting surface. Lay template B on top of your square, aligning the 2 straight edges of the template with the corner of the square, and trim along the curve. Repeat to **make 4** quarter-circles of fabric A, **make 2** quarter-circles of fabric B, and **make 2** quarter-circles of fabric C. **1D**

2 make drunkard's path units

Pair a fabric A quarter-circle with a fabric F corner piece. Fold each piece in half on the diagonal and finger press to mark the midway point of each curved edge. Place the quarter-circle on top of the corner piece, right sides facing, and finger pressed centers aligned. Pin at the midway point and at both ends of the seam allowance. **2A**

Stitch the 2 pieces together along the curve. Use your fingers to ease in the fullness around the curve and avoid stretching the fabric as you sew. Press the seam allowance towards the corner piece to complete the unit. **Make 4**. **2B**

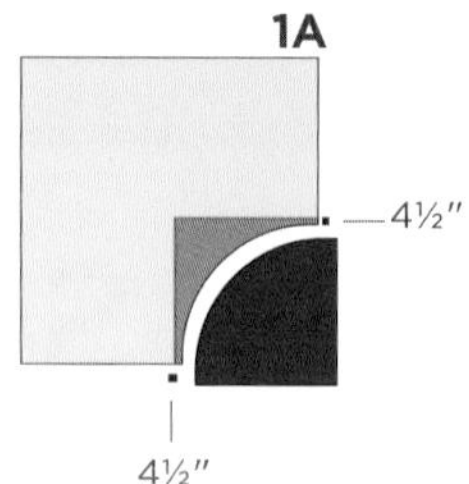

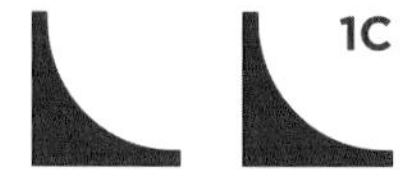

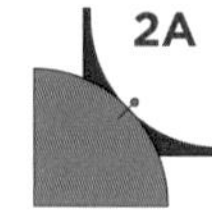

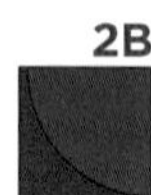

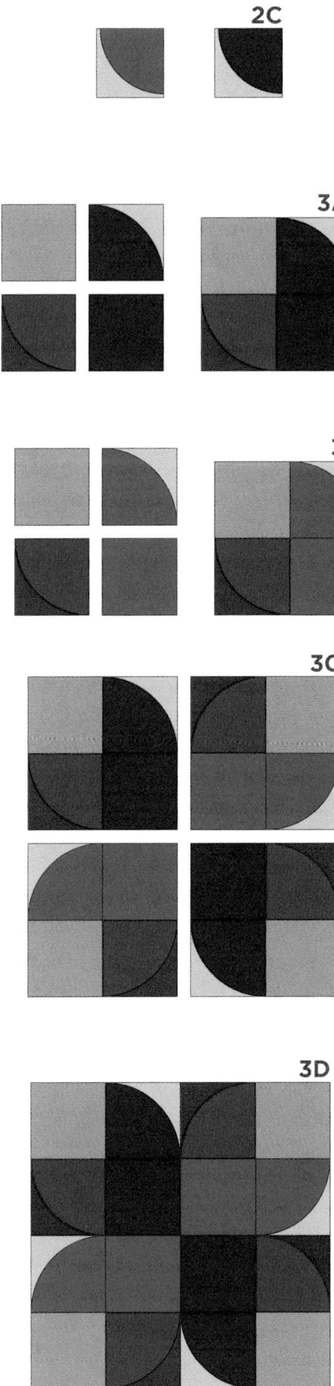

Repeat to **make 2** units using the fabric B quarter-circles and fabric H corner pieces and **make 2** units using the fabric C quarter-circles and fabric H corner pieces. **2C**

3 block construction

Select (1) 4½" fabric D square, 1 C/H unit, 1 A/F unit, and (1) 4½" fabric C square and arrange them as shown. Sew the units together in rows. Press the seam allowances in opposite directions. Nest the seams and sew the rows together to complete 1 A quadrant. **Make 2**. **3A**

Select (1) 4½" fabric D square, 1 B/H unit, 1 A/F unit, and (1) 4½" fabric B square and arrange them as shown. Sew the units together in rows. Press the seam allowances in opposite directions. Nest the seams and sew the rows together to complete 1 B quadrant. **Make 2**. **3B**

Arrange the 4 quadrants in 2 rows of 2 as shown. Notice the placement and orientation of each quadrant. **3C**

Sew the quadrants together in rows. Press the seam allowances in opposite directions. Nest the seams and sew the rows together to complete the Morning Glory block. **3D**

Morning Glory Block Size:
16½" unfinished, 16" finished

4 block border

Sew a 2½" fabric A square to both ends of a 2½" x 16½" fabric D border rectangle. Press towards the rectangle. **Make 2** long borders. **4A**

Sew a border rectangle to both sides of the Morning Glory block. Press towards the rectangle. Sew a long border to the top and bottom of the block. Press towards the borders. **4B 4C**

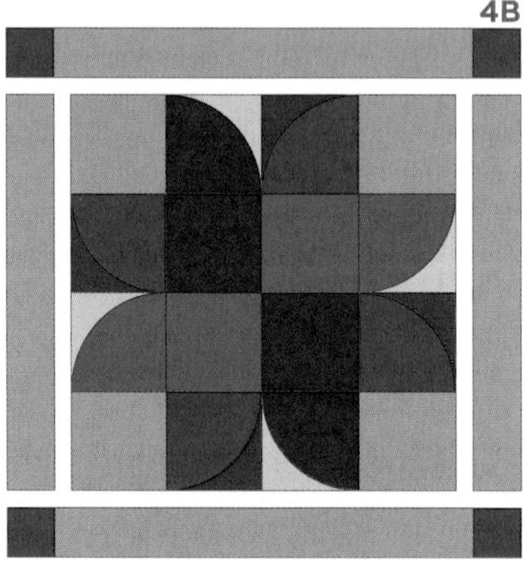

Bordered Morning Glory Size:
20½" unfinished, 20" finished

DARK STUDIO STAR

5 cut

- From the (2) 10" fabric A squares, cut (4) 2½" strips across the width of each.
  - Subcut a **total of (16)** 2½" x 4½" rectangles.

- From (2) 10" fabric B squares, cut (4) 2½" strips across the width of the square. You will have a **total of (8)** 2½" strips.

- From (1) 10" fabric B square, cut (1) 2½" strip across the width. Set the remainder of the square aside.
  - Subcut the strip into a **total of (4)** 2½" squares.

- From the (4) 10" fabric F squares, cut (4) 2½" strips across the width of each square.

- Subcut 8 strips into (4) 2½″ squares each for a **total of 32**.
- You will have a **total of (8)** 2½″ strips remaining.

6 block construction

Sew a fabric B strip to a fabric F strip. Press. **Make 8**. **6A**

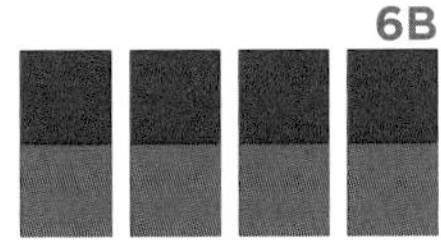

Cut each strip set into 2½″ increments to create 2-patch units. **Make 32**. **6B**

Sew a 2½″ x 4½″ fabric A rectangle to a 2-patch unit as shown. Press. **6C**

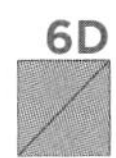

Fold (32) 2½″ fabric F squares once on the diagonal. Press to crease. **6D**

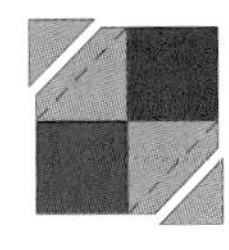
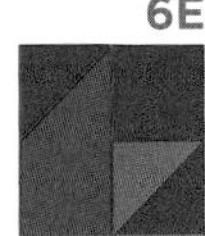

Place a creased fabric F square on 2 corners of the unit as shown and sew each in place on the creased diagonal. Trim the excess fabric away ¼″ from the seam line, then open and press. **Make 16** corner units. **6E**

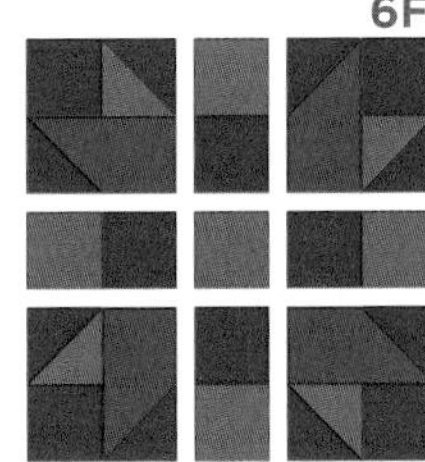

Arrange 4 corner units, (4) 2-patch units, and (1) 2½″ fabric B square as shown. Be aware of the direction the corner units are placed. **6F**

Sew the units together in rows. Press each row towards the 2-patch units. Nest the seams and sew the rows together. Press. **Make 4**. **6G**

Dark Studio Star Block Size:
10½″ unfinished, 10″ finished

LIGHT STUDIO STAR

7 cut

- From the (4) 10″ fabric G squares, cut (4) 2½″ strips across the width of each.
  - Subcut 8 strips into (4) 2½″ squares each for a **total of 32**.
  - You will have a **total of (8)** 2½″ strips remaining.
- From the (2) 10″ fabric J squares, cut (4) 2½″ strips across the width of each square.
  - Subcut a **total of (16)** 2½″ x 4½″ rectangles.
- From (2) 10″ fabric L squares, cut (4) 2½″ strips across the width of each square. You will have a **total of (8)** 2½″ strips.
- From (1) 10″ fabric L square, cut (1) 2½″ strip across the width. Set the remainder of the square aside
  - Subcut the strip into **total of (4)** 2½″ squares.

8 block construction

Sew a fabric L strip to a fabric G strip. Press. **Make 8**. **8A**

Cut each strip set into 2½″ increments to create 2-patch units. **Make 32**. **8B**

8A

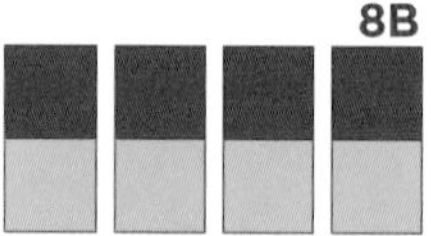
8B

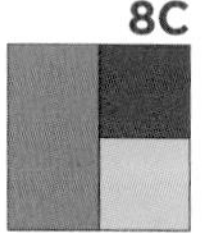
8C

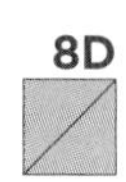
8D

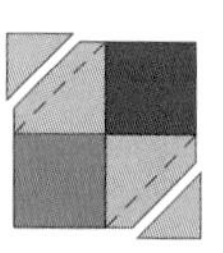

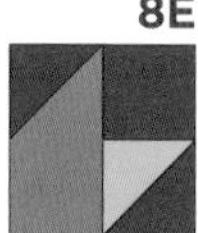
8E

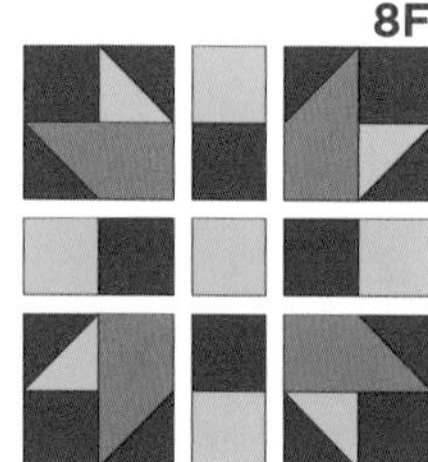
8F

8G

Sew a 2½″ x 4½″ fabric J rectangle to a 2-patch unit as shown. Press. **8C**

Fold (32) 2½″ fabric G squares once on the diagonal. Press to crease. **8D**

Place a creased fabric G square on 2 corners of the unit as shown and sew each in place on the creased diagonal. Trim the excess fabric away ¼″ from the seam line, then open and press. **Make 16** corner units. **8E**

Arrange 4 corner units, (4) 2-patch units, and (1) 2½″ fabric L square as shown. Be aware of the direction the corner units are placed. **8F**

Sew the units together in rows. Press each row towards the 2-patch units. Nest the seams and sew the rows together. Press. **Make 4** blocks. **8G**

Light Studio Star Block Size:
10½″ unfinished, 10″ finished

the STOLEN *stitches*

PART ONE:

THE SECRECY OF QUILTERS

a fiction novella, in six parts ***written by Hillary Doan Sperry***

hillarysperry.com

MISSOURI 1860

"Won't you just tell me his name?" Abigail asked, pulling the cream thread tight on her soon-to-be monogram.

"You know I can't." Lucy insisted.

"But I'm your best friend." Abigail was pouting but it was only an act. Until the previous month she had thought she was the only one with marriage prospects but then she'd found Lucy's letter. It had fallen out of Lucy's pocket and it was so romantic. Lucy had been seeing someone in secret for nearly as long as Abigail had been engaged to her Walter.

Well, mostly engaged. Their parents had set up the arrangement the previous year and while an engagement was assumed, Walt hadn't yet proposed.

"What if it doesn't work out? I'll need to know who to avoid." Abigail tried to focus while her friend laughed. It was nice to finally be able to talk. Lucy'd been so angry when Abigail had confronted her, showing her the letter. But over the weeks she'd relaxed, her anger shifting to fear and finally acceptance. It wouldn't be long before Lucy would be ready to tell her who wrote the letter.

Abigail took a moment to admire the large 'M' on the corner of the large linen tablecloth. It was a shame Lucy had insisted Abigail embroider her own monograms. Lucy was by far the better seamstress, but she said it would mean more.

The 'M' curled beautifully. Though the satin stitching was a touch loose, and the knotted border didn't look as pristine as it did when Lucy made them, it was still nice.

Lucy's fingers flew over a row of intricate florals, her nose deep in her work. Abigail narrowed her eyes. "You still haven't answered me. I should know who he is before you're engaged."

A pretty shade of pink rose in Lucy's cheeks and her stitches slowed. Abigail dropped her tablecloth staring at what was nigh to a confession. "You're blushing! Lucy Fairbanks. Has he asked you to marry him?"

"Don't be ridiculous! Of course not and it's no wonder I'm blushing. You would be too if I suggested you were to wed someone special." Lucy bit her lip, hesitating, and returned to her work.

"Someone special." Abigail giggled, "You mean Walter." Lucy didn't look up and Abigail swooned at the thought of her future husband. "Surely he'll ask me soon. Mrs. Walter Manor. It's so romantic."

"It's not always about romance," Lucy said, her voice gentle, willing the flowers on her cloth to take shape.

Abigail would never be Lucy, but it was enough to be her friend. She tapped Lucy's knee and grinned. "Don't pretend your situation isn't romantic too. Clandestine meetings, a secret lover. I bet it's one of the railroad workers and your father would never approve."

Lucy didn't even look up. "It's not one of the rail men. I thought you knew me better than that. They're so brazen."

This time Abigail didn't respond. She should agree with her friend, but there were a few of the men she'd happened upon in the general store with fair manners and more than fair looks. She wouldn't have minded a clandestine meeting or two with one of them. But then there was Walt.

She picked up her needle and sighed. If Abigail could get Walt to engage in a few clandestine meetings, with a few more stolen kisses, maybe he'd finally make things official.

"Besides," Lucy interrupted Abigail's thoughts with her own. "You've known him for years. It's just that there are—"

"Complications. I know." Abigail turned back to her work, tired of trying to sway her friend to see things her way. "It doesn't matter anyway. But you had better be ready to marry when Walter finally asks me. We'll have a double wedding and live next door to each other and it will be wonderful."

Lucy's smile faltered. She nodded then pulled her fabric to her face again. Abigail huffed, the corner Lucy was finishing didn't seem to be any more intricate than the rest of the tablecloth. Why wouldn't she talk about her young man.

"Is everything all right?" Abigail narrowed her eyes. What if this young man that she'd 'known for years' wasn't one of the upstanding young men in town after all? It would explain why Lucy'd kept the relationship a secret, even from her.

"You won't let him run off with you, right?" Abigail pressed further. "All our plans ... I'm still going to be at your wedding, won't I?"

"Of course," Lucy burst, "it's not like that. Walt would never—" Lucy's hand flew to her mouth. "I didn't mean—I wasn't supposed to say—" Lucy jumped out of her seat like she might run from the room.

Abigail grabbed her friend's hand, the needle falling from her fingers and swinging like a threaded pendulum, counting very long seconds of silence. "What did you just say?"

Lucy started to shake, tears forming crystal beads of pain in her eyes. "Nothing. I didn't say anything."

"But you did. You said Walt would never ... what? Run off with you?" Lucy was crying now. "He wouldn't. I'm so sorry."

"Of course he wouldn't. I'm going to marry Walter Manor. We're embroidering my dowry."

Lucy's skin was painted in red and white sunbursts around Abigail's grip. She was holding Lucy too tightly and had to force herself to let go. As soon as Lucy was free, her hands flew to her face, covering the emotion. "I'm so sorry. We were only friends. It wasn't until the arrangement that we knew we wanted to be more. I didn't mean to hurt you. I'm so sorry."

Abigail's burning anger left no room for forgiveness. The tablecloth fell from her lap as she stood and walked to the door, holding it open for her friend. "Not sorry enough."

PRESENT DAY

The hum of women's voices accented with laughter and clinking dishes made Jenny's day. It was the soundtrack to a party. Hamilton's old baseball field had grown over with grass and was laid out with more than a dozen patchwork quilts. The result appeared to be an even larger quilt with multi-colored blocks and grass-green sashings. Members of the local quilt guild mingled and passed each other on their way to and from the food tables at the back.

The quilts had been a last minute addition after the springtime weather had expressed its volatility and changed from sunshine to rain the evening before the picnic. With only a few hours' notice, and Jenny's insistence that quilts were made to be used and loved, Loretta, the guild president, put out the call for everyone's most sturdy quilts, and the guild members responded.

Despite the soggy ground the park glowed with sunshine and vibrant color, welcoming the group to gather and enjoy. Cherry hadn't yet arrived and Jenny crossed the quilted ground toward her friends Bernie and Dotty. The two women were sisters and as different as you could imagine wherever they went quilting and fun followed.

The women huddled in the corner of the park near Loretta, her short white hair a contrast to Bernie's long gray braids and Dotty's curls. Bernie pinched the bridge of her nose rubbing the skin beneath the arch of her glasses. Jenny paused, she knew that gesture. Something was bothering Bernie.

Jenny had almost reached them when Loretta threw her hands in the air and started digging in a large tote bag. Dotty gasped as Loretta flung fabric and quilt pieces from the bag and the women scrambled to catch them.

"It's not here." Loretta's voice rose above the crowd and Jenny quickened her pace. "I told you, it's gone! My grandmother's tablecloth is gone! Someone stole it!"

"It probably fell out of your bag?" Dotty suggested, gathering a pile of discarded fabric and quilts.

"It didn't fall out. It's a hand stitched, pre-Civil War era embroidery."

"Yes." Bernie sounded more annoyed than her sister. "I think we could all quote its heritage by now. You've been telling us how special that cloth is for a month. Ever since we decided we'd theme this month's quilt guild meeting."

"Well, that's how I know I wouldn't just drop it. It's the oldest piece here. It should be in a museum. Not at a park with thieving guild members and a forgetful owner." Loretta started alternately wringing her hands and covering her mouth.

Jenny leaned down stacking a few of the quilted pieces and held up a small embroidery. "This is lovely."

It was a small square, likely a napkin with a monogrammed 'M' in the corner. The letter curled through a string of florals. A tiny knotted border decorated the last swooping arch like a shadow.

Loretta's hand currently hovered over her lips. "That's a companion piece to the tablecloth. My husband's great-great grandmother made them with a friend, according to the stories. Both their last names started with M so the monogram matched. The Milburn family."

The scowl on Loretta's face only increased the sense of frustration. Folding the cloth and returning it, Jenny inquired, "Your families aren't friends anymore?"

"Not when they try to reclaim them every few years. Someone comes around claiming that the linens belong to their family. But I won't give them up." She shook her head and looked up at the women surrounding her. "I've never wanted to see a Milburn so much in my life. If any of them were here, I'd know exactly who took it."

"Why don't we make an announcement to see if anyone here has seen it? Maybe it was an accident." Jenny's concern echoed Loretta's in a gentler way.

Loretta's head popped up, "Yes. We'll announce it and get everyone looking for which of these thieving women took my family tablecloth."

And she was back. Jenny's lips pinched into a straight line as she forced a smile. "That's a good idea, Bernie, would you say something?" then in a softer voice she added, "Maybe leave out the 'thieving women' part."

Bernie chuckled and disappeared.

"You don't understand." Loretta insisted, shaking a handkerchief at them. "I knew I shouldn't have brought them. I saw an antique road show where they priced several vintage cloths like mine. With its history, not to mention its companion pieces, it's worth several thousand dollars."

"Where did you last have your tablecloth? Did anyone show a particular interest in it?" Jenny hoped there was a simple solution. Loretta's eyes grew wide, "Yes. There was a woman asking questions about it ... Kelly? She left right after the luncheon started."

Jenny started at Kelly's name. Kelly Bruno had been a member of the quilt guild since her first baby was born six years ago. She now had two young children and Jenny couldn't imagine her trying to steal Loretta's famed heirloom.

Loretta fanned herself as she focused on the unsuspecting woman. "She talked to me about where it was from. I even showed her where I kept it, oh my, and then I asked her to watch it while I fixed my luncheon plate. Oh no, I left it in the hands of a thief. Oh my heart."

continued on page 110

WHAT'S A QUILT WORTH?

Do you remember the first quilt that was ever given to you? Maybe it was a baby quilt or a wedding gift. Maybe it was always on your bed growing up and you never knew who made it. But, wherever that first quilt came from, somebody did actually make it. They may have even created it especially with you in mind. They selected the fabrics with care, stitched it by hand or by machine using hours of their precious time, and then bound it and gave it away as a gift. Whether or not we know the origins of our first quilt, we know it has value.

As we look back on quilts that have surrounded us throughout our lives, it may only then occur to us what an incredible gift a quilt is. Block's own Creative Director, Christine Ricks, recalls such an experience. She presented a lecture entitled, "Quilts Are Valued," during QuiltCon 2021 and explains:

"My introduction to quilting came by way of my grandmother, Zola. She loved to make quilts for her grandkids. She made a lot of quilts. She had a lot of grandkids. She made them all for her grandkids when they got married, or went to college, or graduated from high school. They were mostly utilitarian quilts ... simple piecing and any fabric would do. We got quilts from cut up shirts, suits, polyester pants, whatever she could find. She was using what she had and making something with it. She most definitely came from that generation of 'make do'."

"The sad part about this story is, I was never influenced by her quilting efforts as a young girl. I didn't think about the time and effort that went into these blankets. I received one of her quilts when I graduated from high school and I don't even have it anymore. I have no idea where it went. Do you have a story like this? Did your mother, grandmother, neighbor, aunt, or friend quilt? Did you realize what that gift was? Or maybe you didn't realize, like myself, until much later how much you valued that work and time and effort on your behalf."

Even though Christine experienced a feeling of loss by initially not understanding the value of the quilt her grandmother made her, she has since gained a deep appreciation for quilting that has benefitted many more people than just herself. She continues to guide Block Magazine as a person who values quilting and it comes through in her efforts. We have a feeling Grandmother Zola would be more than proud.

It's never too late to gain an appreciation for quilting. With those who have gone on before us leaving behind their handmade treasures, we can move forward with a desire to help future generations understand this labor of love and pass it on.

WHY DO WE VALUE QUILTING?

There are many physical reasons why quilts have value. The cost of the materials, time, and effort alone would be a revelation to many who have never quilted before, but we know the worth of quilts goes much deeper than that.

The creativity and the thought that goes into quilts takes it beyond a sum of the parts it was made from to a value that may only be perceived by a select few.

Often, it is only by going through the process of making a quilt ourselves that we begin to understand its real value. And isn't that the way it is for many other things as well? We attempt to grow our own vegetables in the backyard instead of purchasing them at a store and end up spending double or even triple what we would on tomatoes by the pound to finally pick a bunch of ripe, juicy tomatoes right off the vine and we feel deep satisfaction after a summer of endless watering and weeding. The process of quilting is suddenly not lost on us after stitching up one of our own creations and each quilt we view after that moment becomes much more valuable to us as a result.

Being creative also has its own reward. Expressing our creativity through quilting brings greater peace and happiness in to our lives. We can also teach others how to quilt and see the happiness it brings into their lives. Quilts are physical objects that are more than just beautiful, they're also incredibly useful. You can literally wrap yourself or a loved one up in a quilt when you're finished with it. You can't do that with a book or a picture. Quilts are different in that way. They're a tactile artform that gives comfort. And beyond creating to bring ourselves happiness, gifting quilts to others brings joy as we selflessly share our talents and our love.

THE REAL COST OF QUILTING

For many, quilting is a labor of love that's hard to put a price tag on, but that doesn't mean we can't or shouldn't. Here's a common scenario. Someone spies one of our beautiful quilts, gets a gleam in their eye and asks, "Do you sell your quilts?" We laugh nervously, smile, and say something like, "It's only a hobby. I couldn't possibly sell one of my quilts." The question of how much one of our quilts might cost catches us completely off guard. It's genuinely a tough question to answer. We don't want to say yes without a second thought and then sell one of our precious quilts for a meager sum. We might be afraid to quote a price that seems too high to the person asking. And maybe we don't want to sell our quilts at all.

If this question makes you uncomfortable, you're probably like many quilters out there who have a deep love for quilting, but aren't sure they want to put a price on their passion. The reality is, most quilters are hesitant to express the value of their quilts and why is that?

Making a quilt is a work of heart. From selecting the fabric to choosing a pattern, cutting and piecing, basting, quilting it all together, and stitching on the binding, the work that goes into making your masterpiece could take days or it could take years. When we give quilts, we're not only giving something of great worth, we're giving our time, because quilts don't happen overnight.

The talent it takes to create a quilt doesn't just happen either. People who quilt take years to hone their skills enough to become adept at choosing colors and patterns that work together. Learning more advanced techniques takes even more time. From the most basic skills like pressing and keeping a consistent ¼" seam to more intricate skills like appliqué and hand quilting, clearly not just anyone can make a quilt.

A LABOR OF LOVE

Knowing this, how can we better communicate the value of our quilts to others? We can begin by being honest. Don't explain away your hard work by saying it was easy. Tell people how long you worked on your creation. Point out the intricate details. Tell them how you labored over design decisions. Express the care and attention you put into your project. If you're so inclined, keep a quilting journal, take pictures of each step, and even post about your creative process on social media. People might be surprised to know what goes into making a quilt from start to finish. When others are able to appreciate the process, the end result takes on a whole new meaning.

But really, when it comes down to it, the point of asking "What's a Quilt Worth?" is to cause us all to think twice about the value we place on our work and the work of others; to truly recognize the importance of what we create and help educate everyone about the value of quilts. If we want others to value what we do, we must also value what we do!

YOUR QUILTS HAVE VALUE

Quilting is a highly personal artform. It's an expression of your creativity and your emotion. If you choose to put a price on your creation, make sure it's what you feel is right and avoid giving in to pressure from others. Tell them what it's worth and be proud of your marvelous work. If you don't want to sell what you make, that's more than okay, too. But always remember that your quilts have value.

MAKE A NAME FOR YOURSELF

Chances are, the quilts you've enjoyed all your life have no name on them. And, historically, we know that "anonymous" was often a woman. It's time to break with this nameless tradition and make our work known. Be proud of your creations! Sign your name to your masterpiece and say who made that beautiful quilt. There are many ways to label quilts, but no matter how you do it, here is some important information to include on your quilt label: your name, the name of the quilt pattern, when it was made, who it was made for, and the occasion. Be sure to always use a permanent fabric marker and stitch it on securely! And who says your name has to be on the back of your quilt? Why not on the front? Painters don't sign their names on the back of the canvas, so why should we?

- Use a blank fabric label panel. Cut out a label, write on it with a permanent fabric marker, and stitch it onto your quilt.
- Have personalized labels made. Creating your own custom label is easier than you might imagine. You can have sew-on or iron-on labels made.
- Use a scrap of fabric to create a label. Stitch it into the binding or into a corner of the quilt as a finishing touch. You can also attach it to your quilt with fusible interfacing and stitch down the raw edge.
- Write directly on the quilt using a permanent fabric marker. Some even hand embroider their names onto their quilts. What a beautiful idea!
- Embroider your label and attach it to your quilt. There are many wonderful embroidery machines now and adding a personalized label is easier than ever.

Just Wing It

If you're looking for a quilt to help your imagination take flight, go ahead and just wing it. Pairs of pretty wings fly across this quilt in different directions to add interest to this modern design, but you can turn them any which way you desire! It would look beautiful in prints or solids. But no matter how you create it, this quilt's definitely for the birds!

MATERIALS

QUILT SIZE
57″ x 64″

BLOCK SIZE
7½″ unfinished, 7″ finished

QUILT TOP
1 package of 10″ print squares

INNER BORDER
½ yard

OUTER BORDER
1¼ yards

BINDING
¾ yard

BACKING
3¾ yards or 2½ yards of 108″ wide

OTHER
Missouri Star Quilt Co. Large Wing Template

SAMPLE QUILT
Fleurs by Michel Design Works for Northcott Fabrics

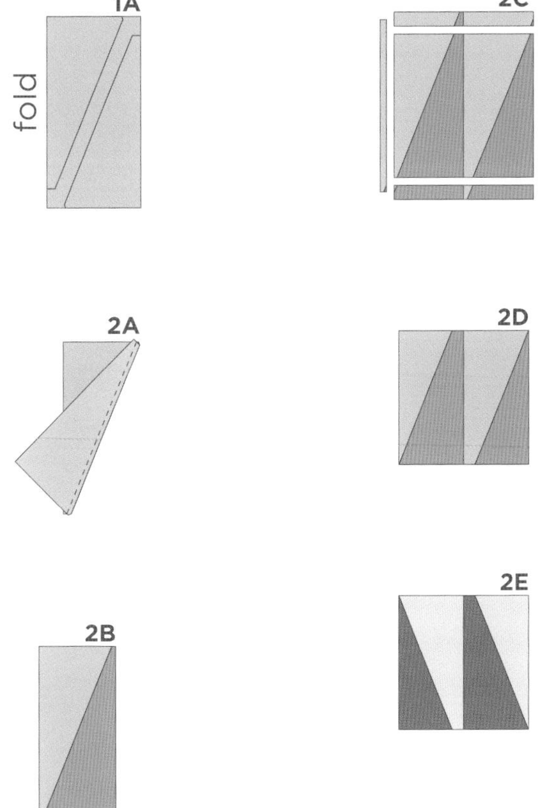

1 cut

Fold each 10″ print square in your package in half. Place the template in 1 corner and cut around the perimeter. Rotate the template 180° and place it in the opposite corner. Cut around the template again. Notice that each square yields 2 pairs of matching pieces that have opposite slants. Keep the pieces organized in matching pairs with the same slant. **1A**

2 block construction

Select 2 different pairs of matching wings. Place 1 wing from each pair with right sides facing and sew along the slanted edge, as shown. Press to 1 side. **Make 2**. **2A 2B**

Sew the 2 units together as shown. Press. Trim to 7½″. **2C**

Make 42 blocks—half will have mirrored slants. **2D 2E**

Block Size: 7½″ unfinished, 7″ finished

3 arrange & sew

Refer to diagram **3A** on page 61 to lay out the blocks in **7 rows of 6**. Notice how the blocks are rotated. When you are happy with your arrangement, sew the blocks together in rows. Press in opposite directions. Nest the seams and sew the rows together. Press.

1. Fold a 10″ square in half. Place the template in 1 corner and cut around the template, then rotate it 180° and cut around the template a second time. You will have 2 mirrored pairs of wings. Make 84 pairs.

2. Select 2 pairs of wings and place 1 wing from each pair with right sides facing and the slanted edges aligned. Sew along the slanted edge. Make 2.

3. Open and press the seam allowance of each unit towards the darker fabric.

4. Sew the 2 units together and press. Half of the blocks will have slanted edges that go from the lower left to upper right.

5. Trim the block to 7½″.

6. Half of the blocks will have slanted edges that go from the upper left to lower right. The 2 units that make up the blocks are sewn together and trimmed in the same manner.

1

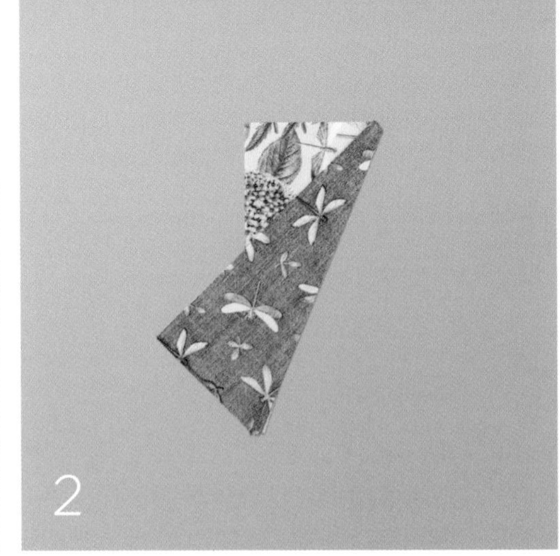
2

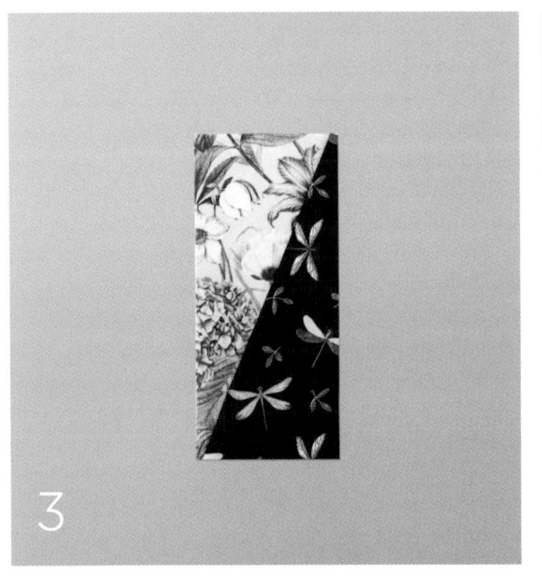
3

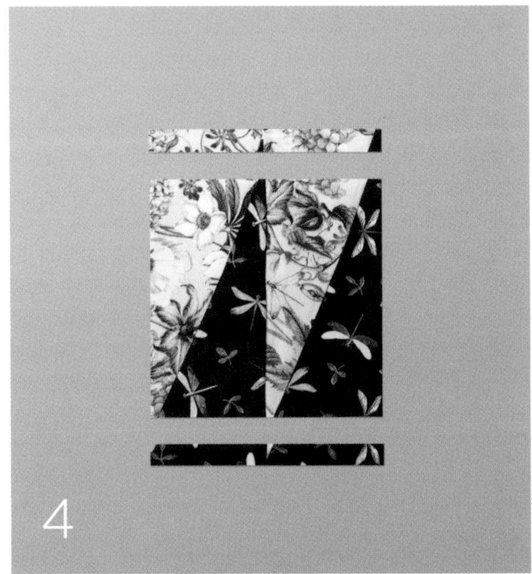
4

5

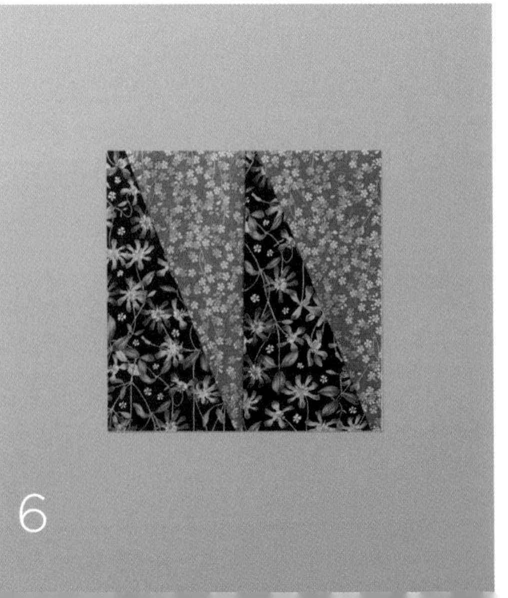
6

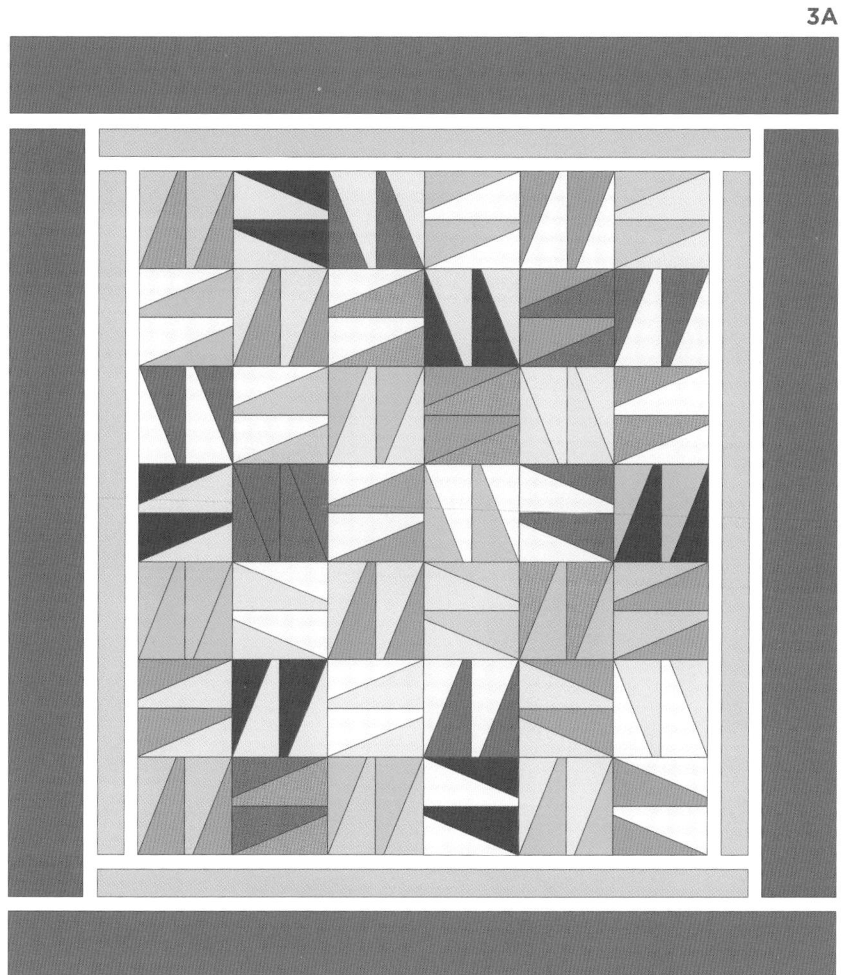

4 inner border

Cut (5) 2½" strips across the width of the inner border fabric. Sew the strips together to make 1 long strip. Trim the borders from this strip. Refer to Borders (pg. 118) in the Construction Basics to measure, cut, and attach the borders. The lengths are approximately 49½" for the sides and 46½" for the top and bottom.

5 outer border

Cut (6) 6" strips across the width of the outer border fabric. Sew the strips together to make 1 long strip. Trim the borders from this strip. Refer to Borders (pg. 118) in the Construction Basics to measure, cut, and attach the borders. The lengths are approximately 53½" for the sides and 57½" for the top and bottom.

6 quilt & bind

Layer the quilt with batting and backing, then quilt. After the quilting is complete, see Construction Basics (pg. 118) add binding and finish your quilt.

Lakeview Terrace

Is there anything more lovely than lounging lakeside as the water laps gently on the shore? Capture the movement of the serene waters with Lakeside Terrace. Staggered strips make this quilt design as easy as can be with hardly any pesky points to match up! Water you waiting for? Let's get started!

MATERIALS

QUILT SIZE
83" x 95½"

BLOCK SIZE
10½" x 8" unfinished,
10" x 7½" finished

QUILT TOP
1 roll of 2½" print strips
4 yards of background fabric
- includes inner border

OUTER BORDER
1½ yards

BINDING
¾ yard

BACKING
8¾ yards - vertical seam(s)
or 3 yards of 108" wide

SAMPLE PROJECT
Modern Love by Deborah Edwards and Melanie Samra for Northcott

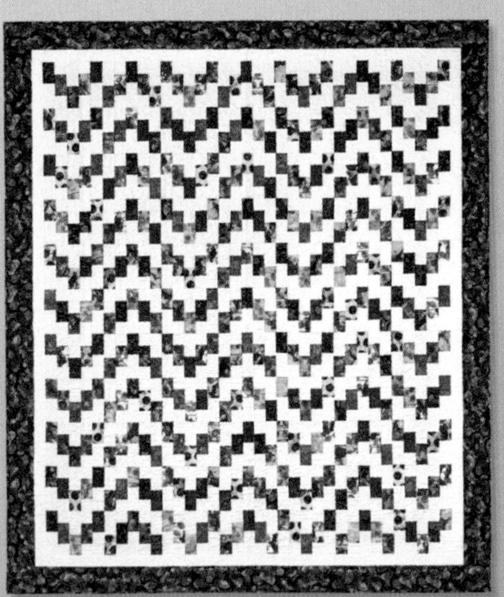

1 cut

From the 2½" print strips, cut 2½" x 4" rectangles. Each strip will yield up to 10 rectangles and a **total of 385** are needed.

From the background fabric, cut (54) 2½" strips across the width of the fabric.

- From 26 of the strips, subcut a **total of (231)** 2½" x 4½" rectangles.
- From 20 of the strips, subcut a **total of (308)** 2½" squares.
- Set 8 of the strips aside for the inner border.

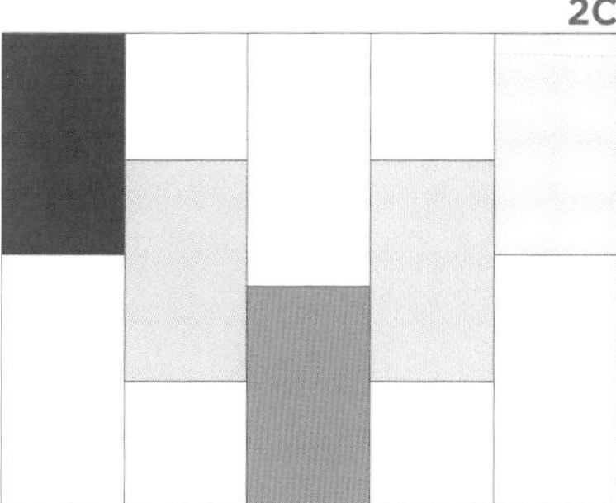

2 sew

Select (5) 2½" x 4" print rectangles, (3) 2½" x 4½" background rectangles, and (4) 2½" background squares.

Sew a background rectangle to the 1 short side of a print rectangle. **Make 3** A units. **2A**

Sew a background square to both short ends of a print rectangle. **Make 2** B units. **2B**

Arrange the 5 units as shown, alternating between A and B units. Notice that the A unit in the center is rotated 180° from the 2 A units on the ends. Sew the units together to form a block and press. **Make 77**. **2C**

Block Size: 10½" x 8" unfinished, 10" x 7½" finished

1 Sew a background rectangle to 1 short side of a print rectangle. Make 3 A units.

2 Sew a background square to both short ends of a print rectangle. Make 2 B units.

3 Arrange the 5 units as shown, alternating between A and B units. Notice that the center A unit is rotated 180° from the A units on the ends.

4 Sew the 5 units together to form the block and press. Make 77 blocks.

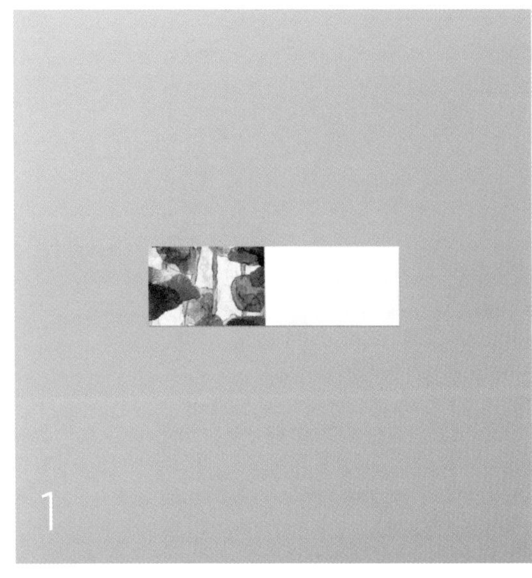

3A

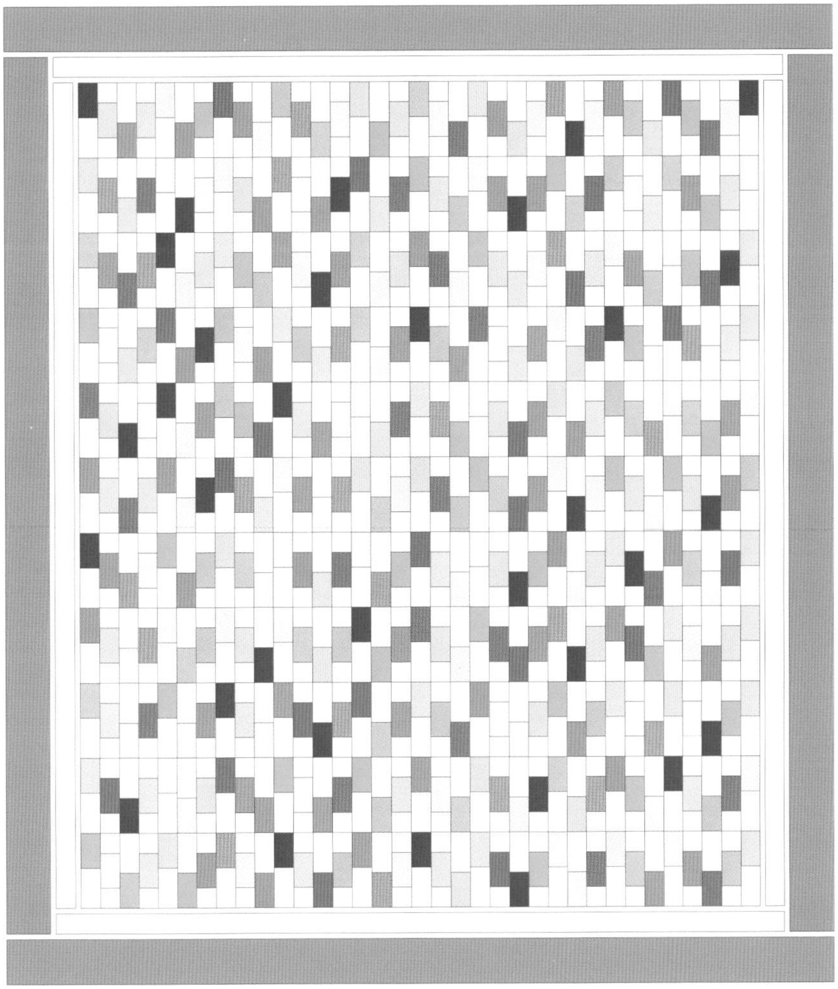

3 arrange & sew

Refer to diagram **3A** to lay out the blocks in **11 rows of 7**. Notice that every other block is rotated 180°. Sew the blocks together in rows. Press in opposite directions. Nest the seams and sew the rows together. Press.

4 inner border

Pick up the (8) 2½" background strips set aside earlier. Sew them together to form a long strip. Cut the inner borders from this strip. Refer to Borders (pg. 118) in the Construction Basics to measure, cut, and attach the borders. The strip lengths are approximately 83" for the sides and 74½" for the top and bottom.

5 outer border

From the outer border fabric, cut (9) 5" strips across the width of the fabric. Sew them together to form a long strip. Cut the outer borders from this strip. Refer to Borders (pg. 118) in the Construction Basics to measure, cut, and attach the borders. The strip lengths are approximately 87" for the sides and 83½" for the top and bottom.

6 quilt & bind

Layer the quilt with batting and backing, then quilt. See Construction Basics (pg. 118) to add binding and finish your quilt.

Lots O' Luck Table Runner

Stitch up a lucky table runner just in time to celebrate St. Patrick's Day in stunning Peacock Garden fabrics. It's sure to give you more good luck than a four-leaf clover! This intricate-looking knot design doesn't require much fabric, but the result is fabulous. Then place it on your table to invite the Leprechauns on over to play.

MATERIALS

PROJECT SIZE
53″ x 21″

BLOCK SIZE
16½″ unfinished, 16″ finished

PROJECT TOP
(2) 2½″ strips or 1 fat quarter each of 4 different prints
½ yard of background fabric

BORDER
½ yard

BINDING
½ yard

BACKING
1¾ yards

SAMPLE PROJECT
Peacock Garden by Studio RK for Robert Kaufman

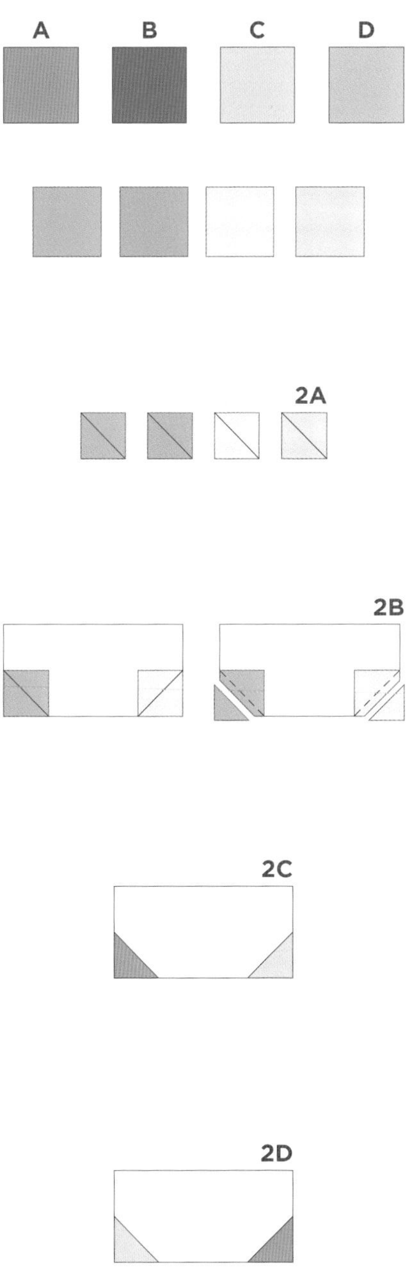

1 cut

Tip: It will be helpful to label the pieces as you cut.

Strip Cutting Directions

From the A and C strips, cut 1 strip of each into (6) 2½″ x 4½″ rectangles and (4) 2½″ squares. From each remaining strip, cut (8) 2½″ squares. You will have a **total of (6)** 2½″ x 4½″ rectangles and a **total of (12)** 2½″ squares of both colors.

From the B and D strips, cut 1 strip of each into (3) 2½″ x 6½″ rectangles, (3) 2½″ x 4½″ rectangles, and (2) 2½″ squares. From each remaining strip, cut (7) 2½″ squares. You will have a **total of (3)** 2½″ x 6½″ rectangles, a **total of (3)** 2½″ x 4½″ rectangles, and a **total of (9)** 2½″ squares of both colors.

Fat Quarter Cutting Directions

From each fat quarter, cut (3) 2½″ strips across the width (20-22″) of the fabric.

From the A and C strips, cut 1 strip of each into (4) 2½″ x 4½″ rectangles. From another strip of each color, cut (2) 2½″ x 4½″ rectangles and (4) 2½″ squares. From each remaining strip, cut (8) 2½″ squares.

From the B and D strips, cut each strip into (1) 2½″ x 6½″ rectangle, (1) 2½″ x 4½″ rectangle, and (3) 2½″ squares.

Note: See totals of each above.

1 Place a marked square on the bottom left and right corners of a 4½" x 8½" background rectangle, right sides facing. Sew on the marked lines. Trim the excess fabric away ¼" from the sewn seam line. Press. Make 3 A/C rectangles, 3 C/A rectangles, 3 B/D rectangles, and 3 D/B rectangles.

2 Sew a 2½" A square to the top of a 2½" x 6½" B rectangle and a 2½" C square to the bottom of a 2½" x 6½" D rectangle as shown. Press. Sew a 2½" x 4½" A rectangle to the top of a 4½" background square and a 2½" x 4½" C rectangle to the bottom of the square. Press.

3 Arrange the 3 units just sewn as shown. Sew the units together and press to complete a center square. Make 3.

4 Sew an A square to the right of a background square. Press. Sew a B rectangle to the bottom of the unit. Press. Make 3 A corner units, B corner units, C corner units, and D corner units.

5 Arrange 1 of each unit in 3 rows of 3 as shown. Top row: A corner unit, B/D rectangle, D corner unit. Middle row: C/A rectangle, center square, A/C rectangle. Bottom row: B corner unit, D/B rectangle, C corner unit.

6 Sew the units together in rows. Press towards the corner units and center square. Nest the seams and sew the rows together to complete the block. Press. Make 3.

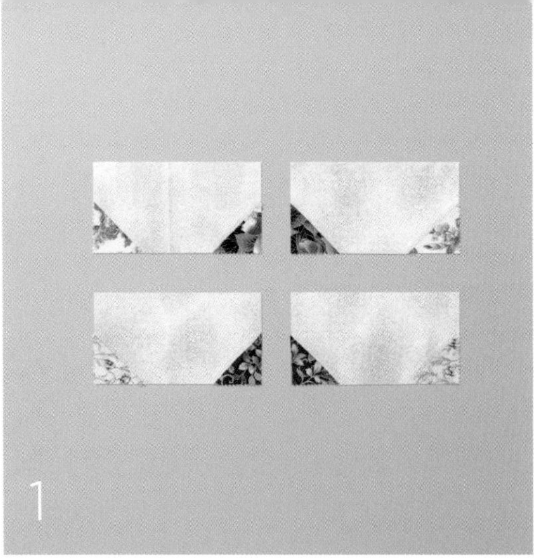

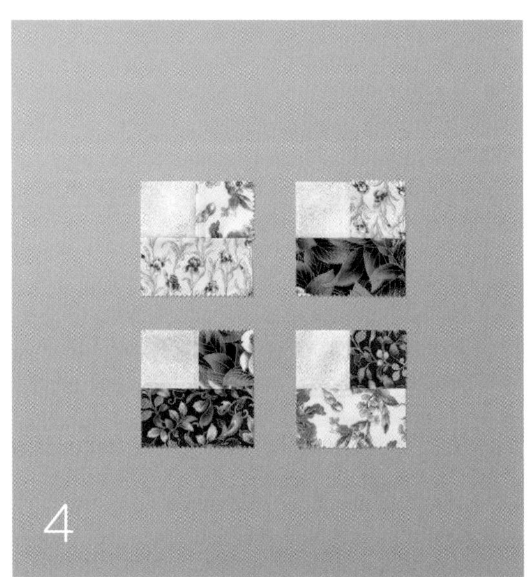

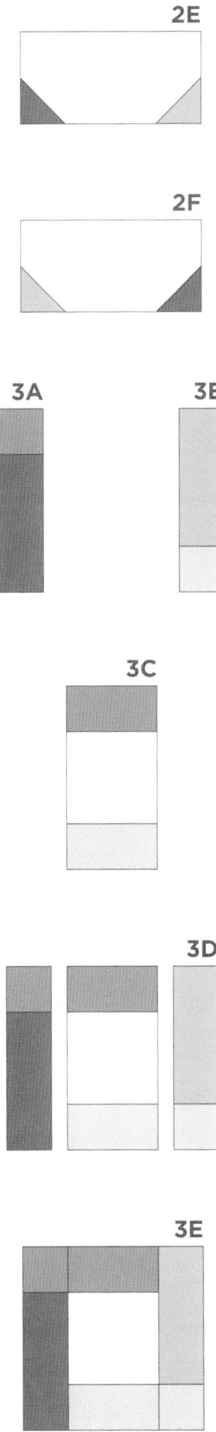

From the background fabric, cut:

- (3) 4½" strips across the width of the fabric. Subcut (4) 4½" x 8½" rectangles and (1) 4½" square from each strip.

- (1) 2½" strip across the width of the fabric. Subcut (12) 2½" squares.

2 snowball corners

Select (6) 2½" squares of each color. Mark a diagonal line on the reverse side of each square. **2A**

Place a marked A square on the bottom left corner of a 4½" x 8½" background rectangle, right sides facing. Place a marked C square on the opposite corner, right sides facing. Notice the angles of the marked squares reflect. Sew on the marked lines. Trim the excess fabric away ¼" from the sewn seam line. **2B**

Press open. **Make 3** A/C rectangles. **2C**

Repeat to snowball another background rectangle, this time with a C square in the bottom left corner and an A square in the bottom right corner. **Make 3** C/A rectangles. **2D**

Repeat again to snowball a background rectangle, with a B square in the bottom left corner and the D square in the bottom right corner. **Make 3** B/D rectangles. **2E**

Repeat to snowball another background rectangle, this time with a D square in the bottom left corner and a B square in the bottom right corner. **Make 3** D/B rectangles. **2F**

3 make the center squares

Gather 3 of each of the following: 2½" A squares, 2½" C squares, 2½" x 4½" A rectangles, 2½" x 4½" C rectangles, 2½" x 6½" B rectangles, 2½" x 6½" D rectangles, and 4½" background squares. Sew a 2½" A square to the top of a 2½" x 6½" B rectangle as shown. Press. **3A**

Sew a 2½" C square to the bottom of a 2½" x 6½" D rectangle as shown. Press. **3B**

Sew a 2½" x 4½" A rectangle to the top of a 4½" background square. Sew a 2½" x 4½" C rectangle to the bottom of the square. Press. **3C**

Arrange the 3 units just sewn as shown. Sew the units together and press to complete a center square. **Make 3**. **3D 3E**

4 make corner units

Use the remaining squares and rectangles and sew an A square to the right of a background square. Press. Sew a B rectangle to the bottom of the unit. Press. Repeat to **make 3** A corner units. **4A**

Sew a B square to the right of a background square. Press. Sew a C rectangle to the bottom of the unit just sewn. Press. Repeat to **make 3** B corner units. **4B**

Sew a C square to the right of a background square. Press. Sew a D rectangle to the bottom of the unit just sewn. Press. Repeat to **make 3** C corner units. **4C**

Sew a D square to the right of a background square. Press. Sew an A rectangle to the bottom of the unit just sewn. Press. Repeat to **make 3** D corner units. **4D**

5 block construction

Arrange 1 of each unit in 3 rows of 3 as shown. The top row will consist of an A corner unit, a B/D rectangle, and a D corner unit. The middle row will consist of a C/A rectangle, a center square, and an A/C rectangle. The bottom row will consist of a B corner unit, a D/B rectangle, and a C corner unit. **5A**

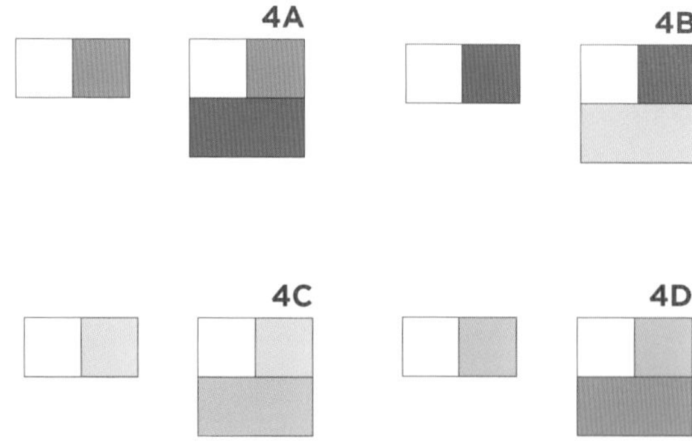

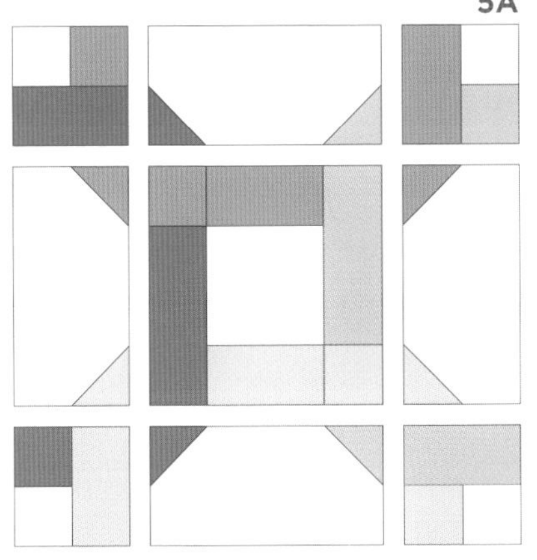

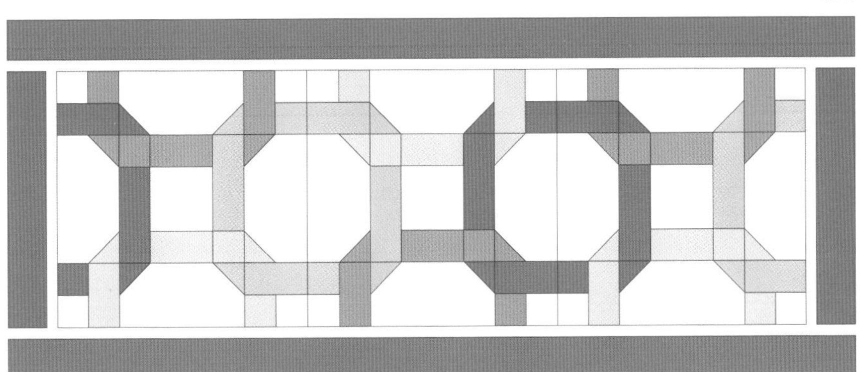

Sew the units together in rows. Press towards the corner units and center square. Nest the seams and sew the rows together to complete the block. Press. **Make 3**. 5B

Block Size: 16½" unfinished, 16" finished

6 arrange & sew

Refer to diagram **6A** as needed to lay out your blocks in **1 row of 3**. The center block will be rotated 180° from the first and last blocks. Sew the blocks together. Press.

7 border

Cut (4) 3" strips across the width of the border fabric. Sew the strips together to make 1 long strip. Trim the borders from this strip. Refer to Borders (pg. 118) in the Construction Basics to measure, cut, and attach the borders. The strips are approximately 16½" for the sides and 53½" for the top and bottom.

8 quilt & bind

Layer the project with batting and backing, then quilt. See Construction Basics (pg. 118) to add binding and finish your project.

little dresses for AFRICA

"I think a hero is any person really intent on making this a better place for all people."
-Maya Angelou

Since it was first founded in 2008, Little Dresses for Africa has been improving the lives of children all across the Continent of Africa, starting in the small village of Ntcheu, Malawi. Founded by Rachel O'Neill, LDFA's primary goal is to encourage self-worth and love in little girls by providing them with simple, yet beautiful, dresses. And not just little girls either. LDFA also has a program called "Britches for Boys," which helps provide quality pants for boys of all ages.

Little Dresses for Africa has gained so much global interest over the years, they've accumulated thousands of devoted volunteers and established dress collection/distribution centers in 97 countries. Through the combined efforts of the organization and their volunteers, LDFA has donated around 9 million dresses! The types of dresses and pants LDFA donates are perfectly easy to make, in fact, the patterns used for the dresses are usually done with pillowcases. This way, little girls get to wear cute and comfortable dresses made of strong, quality fabric. What makes them even more convenient is that children don't have to worry about busted buttons or snagged zippers. Since clothing repairs can be difficult to come by in developing countries, LDFA does not include fasteners in their patterns.

But clothing is just one of many things Little Dresses for Africa has been able to provide. Clean water, education, and community are LDFA's nearest and dearest goals, and monetary donations and distributions of dresses and pants have allowed them to provide these to the people of Malawi and other regions of Africa. They've built two schools in two villages, The Nan Ray School of Learning in Ntcheu, Malawi, and the Jephthah School of Hope in Mataka Village in Malawi. Togetherness and community are often the heart of these tightly-knit villages, which inspired LDFA to construct 2 sewing centers in Malawi!

They've also built 72 wells that have provided clean water for over 180,000 people. By having a well in their village, children are able to spend their days in school instead of walking back and forth from the well to bring water to their households. LDFA's Dignity program has also helped keep young girls in school. Feminine products aren't plentiful in most rural African villages, and their scarcity often keeps young girls in their homes instead of the classroom. But the Dignity program helps supply washable menstrual pads and panties, allowing all girls and women the freedom and comfort they deserve.

The size of any act of kindness has no bearing on the difference it can make. A handmade dress can make one little girl feel powerful, a clean water well can nourish an entire community. The differences between these two kindnesses aren't important, only the everlasting impact they leave. If you want to learn even more about Little Dresses for Africa and Britches for Boys, visit their website at **littledressesforafrica.org** and discover just how needed your heart and sewing skills are.

Solve Quilting Problems WITH SIMPLE MATH

During math class in high school, I spent quite a bit of time doodling in my notebook rather than solving equations. I had the hardest time connecting those abstract concepts to solving real problems in my life back then. But since then, I have come to realize that while I may not have started out with a love of geometry or algebra, I actually use a lot of math in quilting!

Sharpening your math skills can actually improve the quality of your quilting. I used to think accuracy didn't matter much, but have you ever tried sewing together rows of quilt blocks that are just a bit off? Oh boy, those little increments sure add up quickly causing all kinds of problems. When my blocks aren't a consistent size, it's nearly impossible to nest my seams. And I absolutely hate it when I run out of binding right before the end! But a bit of math solves all these pesky quilting problems. Here are a few of the most common problems I encounter and my simple solutions:

SEAMS AREN'T ALIGNING CORRECTLY

Before you begin sewing, cutting your fabric with precision will prevent many problems later on, like seams not lining up. Be sure to use a sharp rotary cutter, a flat cutting mat (if your mat has warped it will not be accurate), and a ruler or template that works well with the way you think. Some rulers have more markings than others—personally, I prefer an uncluttered ruler so I can see what I'm doing! As you cut, whenever possible, measure with your fabric with your ruler and not with your cutting mat. This will ensure greater accuracy. Using precut fabrics will also help your accuracy instantly, as they are already cut to the correct size.

When you start sewing, it's important to do your very best to keep a ¼" inch seam allowance. There's a few ways you can do this: some quilters simply line up their fabric with a piece of blue tape at the right measurement on their machine or use seam guide tape, there's also a handy ¼" foot that will help you keep your seam allowance consistent, and you can also find magnetic and adhesive seam guides for your machine. Whichever method you prefer, figure out what helps you create the most consistent ¼" seam. Once you have that down, you'll discover that your seams nest together wonderfully after they're pressed.

INCONSISTENT BLOCK SIZE

Creating a quilt from your own imagination can be a pleasure when you understand the math of how a quilt comes together. When you start with a quilt block, keep in mind that your block will end up ¼" smaller on all sides because of the seam allowance. Often you'll see in quilt patterns that a block has a "finished size," which means the size your block ends up being once it's sewn into the quilt. Knowing that, you'll want to leave enough room around the edge of your block to show off your design. Always be sure to account for that ¼" seam allowance, otherwise the finished quilt size won't come out right. For example, if your quilt block is 5" square before you sew it, the finished size will be 4½" square after it's sewn together with the other blocks. Remember, a quilt on the design wall looks much larger than a quilt that is completely sewn together.

UNEVEN OR WAVY BORDERS

Wavy borders can be so frustrating! To avoid this, before you cut your border pieces, be sure to measure the length of your quilt top in three different places to ensure greater accuracy. Start measuring 4" in from the edge. After you've measured one side, double that measurement because there are two sides to your quilt. Remember your ¼" seam allowance and add 1" to the width of each border piece. Cut your two side borders and sew them onto your quilt. Then it's time to measure the borders for the top and bottom of your quilt.

Begin by measuring the width of your quilt in three different places as well. Because there is a top and a bottom to the quilt, double that measurement. Then, as always, add on 1" to the width of each of those border pieces to account for the seam allowance. Cut your top and bottom borders and sew them onto your quilt.

NOT HAVING ENOUGH BACKING

Having enough yardage to cover the entire back of a quilt can be a real challenge. You don't want to buy too much and have yards and yards left over, but buying too little is even worse! It's much easier to do the math instead of guessing and get exactly what you need.

- Measure the length and width of your quilt top. If you are going to machine quilt your project, add an extra 8" to both the length and width of your quilt—that's 4" on each side and 4" on the top and bottom. This accounts for any shifting that may occur while quilting.

- Take your measurements, add them both together, and divide it by 36" (one yard).

If your quilt measures narrower than the width of your backing, you can simply cut your backing fabric to the length you need. This is often the case with smaller quilts like baby quilts. But, if your quilt is wider than 42", you'll need to figure out how many fabric widths to piece together and multiply that number by the quilt backing length. Continue on with the next steps and that will be the number of inches of fabric you need to buy.

Wave Goodbye!

Here's another easy way to avoid wavy borders. Before you begin sewing, position your border fabric on top of your quilt and pin it well to prevent distortion and keep the edge flat.

- Determine the number of Widths of Fabric (sometimes abbreviated WOFs) you need for your backing by dividing your width measurement by 40″.
- Cut the fabric to your backing length and piece together with ½″ seam allowances.

If you want to avoid piecing together backing altogether, try special quilt backing fabric that measures 108″ wide instead of using typical 42″ wide fabric.

MATCHING UP BINDING ENDS

Believe me, I have struggled with binding! Getting it right just takes a little know-how and some accurate measurements. Here's how to do it:

1. Measure each of the four sides and add them together. That's the perimeter of your quilt.
2. Add 20″ to your total. To give you enough play to connect your fabric strips.
3. Choose your binding width. We recommend using 2½″ wide strips. Jelly rolls work great here!
4. Divide the total length of binding needed for your quilt by 40″ to allow for room to join strips and trim selvages. This gives you the number of width of fabric strips needed to create your binding.
5. Round up to the nearest whole number of strips. Multiply the number of strips by the width of binding you decided in step 3. That will give you the number of inches required to cut the necessary number of binding strips for your quilt if you want to cut your own strips.
6. Divide the number determined in step 5 by 36″ to calculate the yardage. Round this number up to the next ¼ yard increment and you'll have your total yardage number!

Jan & Jenny's Garden

Jan Patek is a dear friend of mine and I love this quilt we designed together. It's called "Jan and Jenny's Garden." Jan and I have been good friends since the beginning of Missouri Star and I even got her to dress up with me for Quilt Market one year! She lives relatively close to Hamilton and has been a wonderful support to me. Jan is well known for her primitive appliqué and we wanted to create a quilt that combined piecing and needle turn appliqué. Filled with fluttering birds, pinwheel and star flowers, with a scrappy patchwork border on two sides, it's the perfect wall hanging for spring. And if you're new to appliqué, be sure to check out our "Appliqué Like a Pro" tutorials featuring Jan Patek on YouTube. We'll help you get started!

Star Bright

I created this bright, beautiful baby quilt with leftover half-square triangles from another project. If you need a quick, yet stunning baby quilt, this is a wonderful option! It's made with pretty Kaffe Fassett Classic Spots in lovely purples, pinks, and oranges, with a pop of teal. After I made this quilt, I was then inspired to create yet another quilt you may have heard of called "Night Sky" which uses five stars. As we all know, one good quilt leads to another!

A SPOOL IN Love
Quack ON
Quilty AS
Love
sew in Love
A SPOOL IN Love
sew Cute
moda FABRICS + SUPPLIES www.modafabrics.com
FINE TIP FABRIC MARKER AP
FINE TIP FABRIC MARKER AP

Conversation Heart Pillows

MATERIALS

PROJECT SIZE
16" x 16"

PROJECT SUPPLIES
1 package of 5" solid or blender squares
½ yard of background fabric - includes pillow back

OTHER
Missouri Star Half Heart Template
Missouri Star Fabric Markers
Missouri Star Light Fusible Adhesive 17" x 2 yards
PolyFil Fiber

BONUS - SMALL HEART PILLOWS

PROJECT SIZE
5½" x 5½"

PROJECT SUPPLIES
(1) 5" solid or blender square
¼ yard background fabric

OTHER
Missouri Star Half Heart Template
Missouri Star Fabric Markers
Missouri Star Light Fusible Adhesive 17" x 2 yards*
PolyFil Fiber

**At least (1) 4¼" square of fusible adhesive is needed.*

PRACTICE PDF SHEETS
msqc.co/handlettering

1 cut

From the package of 5″ solid squares:

- Select 7 different squares. Cut each square in half both vertically and horizontally for a **total of (28)** 2½″ squares. **1A**

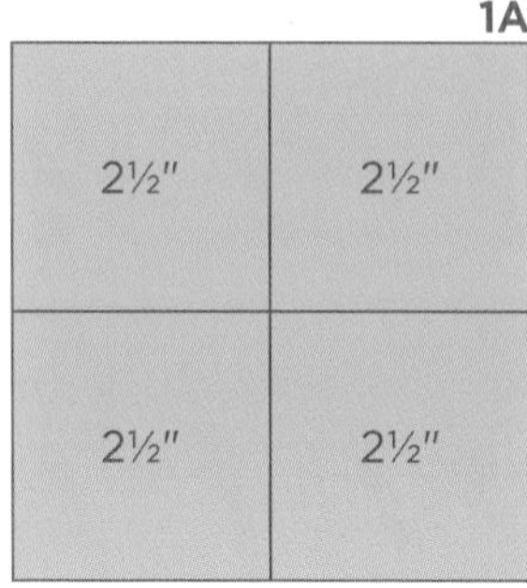

- Set the remaining squares aside for the moment.

From the background fabric:

- Cut (1) 16½″ strip across the width of the fabric.
  - Subcut (1) 16½″ square. **1B**

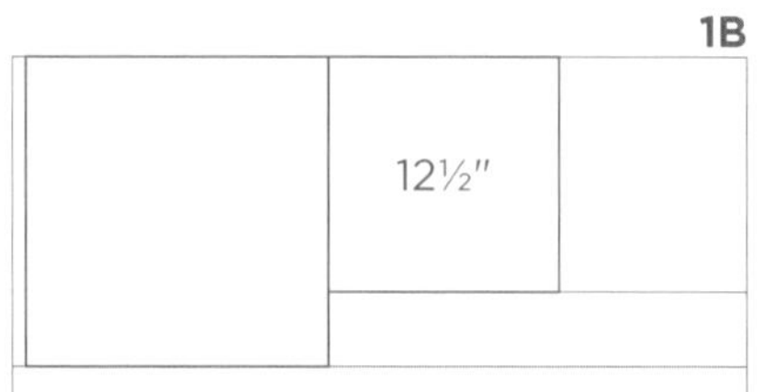

  - From the remainder of the 16½″ strip, subcut a 12½″ strip across the width. Subcut (1) 12½″ square. **1B**

- Set the remaining fabric aside for another project.

From the fusible web:

- Cut (2) 4¼″ strips across the width of the fusible adhesive.
  - Subcut a **total of (5)** 4¼″ squares. **1C**

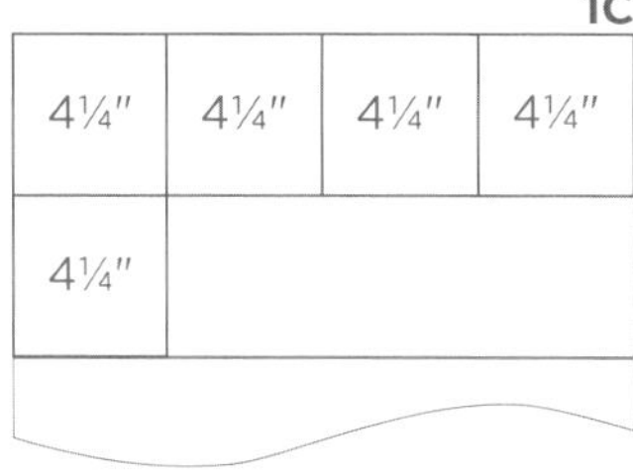

- Set the remaining fusible adhesive aside for the bonus project.

2 trace & cut

Select (5) 5″ squares from the remaining solid squares. Set the remaining squares aside for the bonus project.

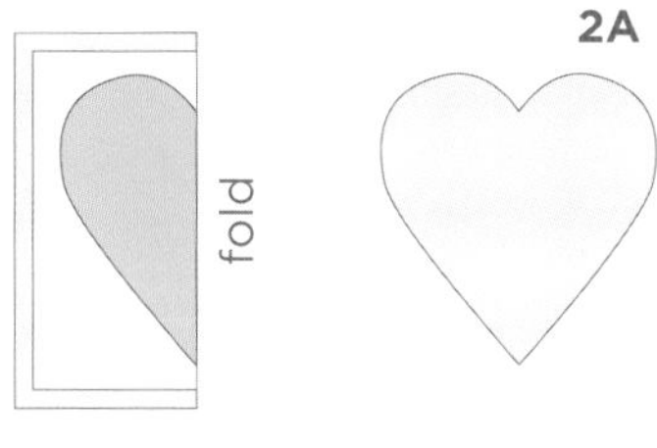

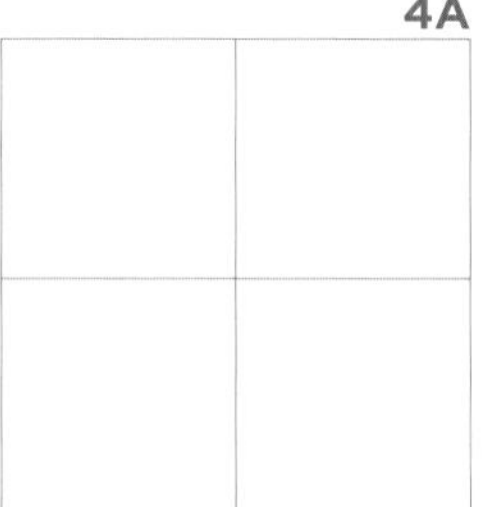

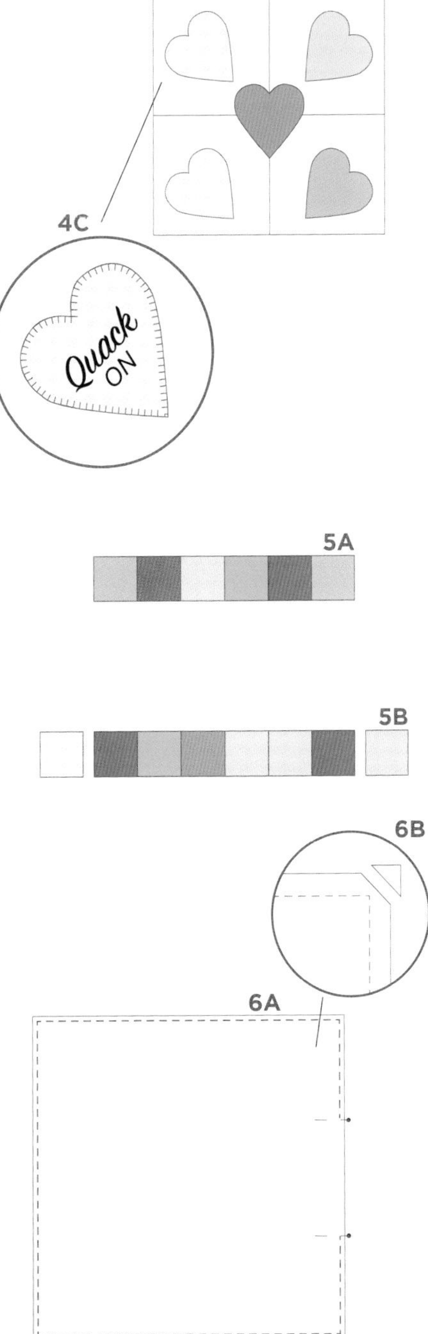

Following the manufacturer's directions, center and adhere the fusible squares on the reverse side of the selected solid squares. Fold 1 fused square in half, right sides together. Lay the template on top with the straight edge along the fold and trace around the curved edge of the template. Keep the square folded and cut along the traced line. **Cut 5** hearts. **2A**

3 write a message

Using a fabric marker, write a message in the center of the hearts. **Note**: For inspiration visit **msqc.co/handlettering** **3A**

4 pillow top

Fold the 12½" background square in half vertically and horizontally to mark the centerlines. Center a heart on top of the background square and place the remaining 4 hearts in each corner as shown. When you're happy with the arrangement, peel off the paper backing from each of the prepared hearts, and follow the manufacturer's instructions to adhere the hearts to the background square. **4A 4B**

After the hearts have been fused to the background square, stitch around the edges of the hearts with a small zigzag, blanket, or decorative stitch. **Tip**: Start your decorative stitches at the bottom point of each heart to keep the pattern repeating evenly. **4C**

5 pieced border

Arrange (6) 2½″ solid squares, alternating colors. Sew the squares together to form a border strip, making any adjustments to the seam allowances necessary to match the length of your pillow top. Press. **Make 4** border strips. **5A**

Sew a 2½″ square to either side of 2 border strips. Press. **5B**

Refer to diagram **5C** to sew a shorter border strip to either side of your pillow top. Press. Sew the longer border strips to the top and bottom of your pillow top. Press.

5C

6 make the pillow

Place the pillow top and the 16½″ square together, right sides facing. With pins, mark a 6″ opening on 1 of the sides. Start by backstitching at a pin, sew around the pillow until you reach the next pin, then backstitch again. Clip the corners. **6A 6B**

Turn right side out. Push the corners out. Press.

At the opening, turn the seam allowance to the inside and hold it taut as you press. This will give you a sewing line to use when you hand stitch the opening closed.

Use Poly-Fil Fiber to stuff the pillow. Close the opening using an invisible hand stitch.

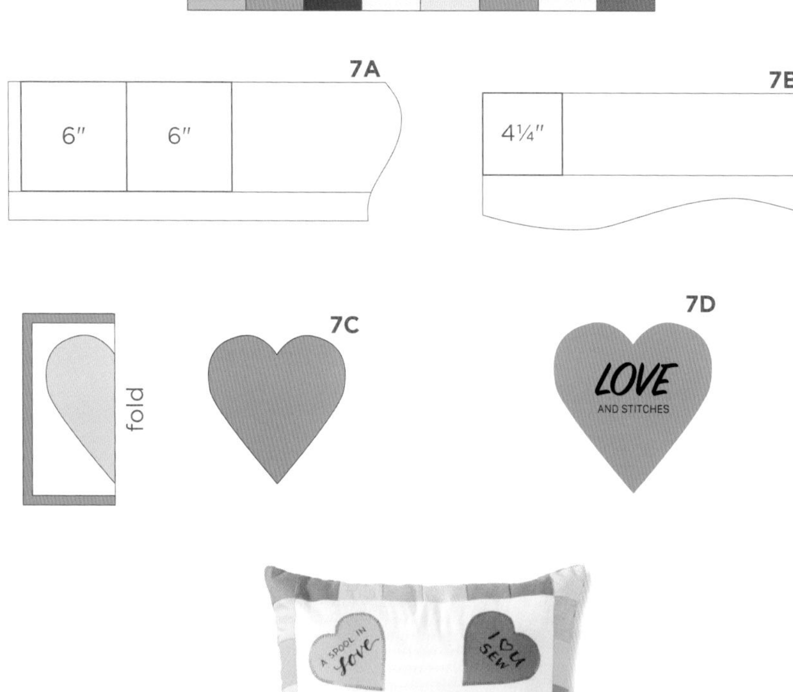

7 bonus small heart pillows

- From the background fabric, cut (1) 6″ strip across the width of the fabric.
  - Subcut (2) 6″ squares. **7A**

- From the fusible web, cut (1) 4¼″ strip across the width of the fabric.
  - Subcut (1) 4¼″ square. **7B**

Follow the previous instructions in sections 2 and 3 to fuse, trace, and cut a heart from the 5″ solid square, then write a message. **7C 7D**

Peel off the paper backing from a prepared heart and discard it. Fold the 6″ background square in half vertically and horizontally to mark the centerlines. Center and adhere the heart on top of a background square. When you're happy with the placement, follow the manufacturer's instructions to adhere the heart to the square.

After the heart has been fused to the background square, appliqué as before with a small zigzag, blanket, or decorative stitch. **7E**

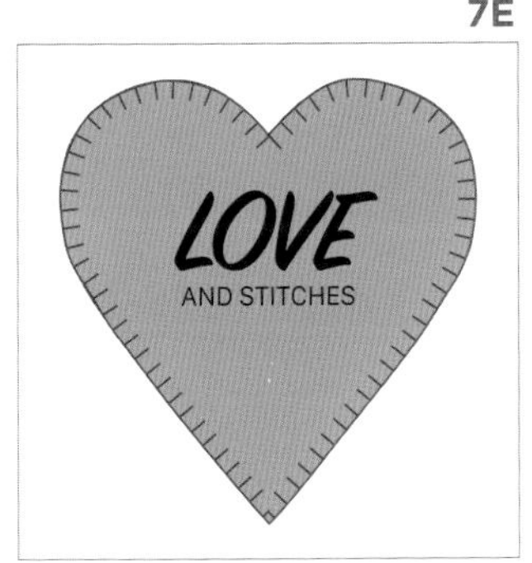

Place the appliquéd heart and the remaining 6″ background square together with right sides facing. With pins, mark about a 3″ opening on 1 of the sides. Start by backstitching at a pin, sew around the pillow until you reach the next pin, then backstitch again. Clip the corners. **7F 7G**

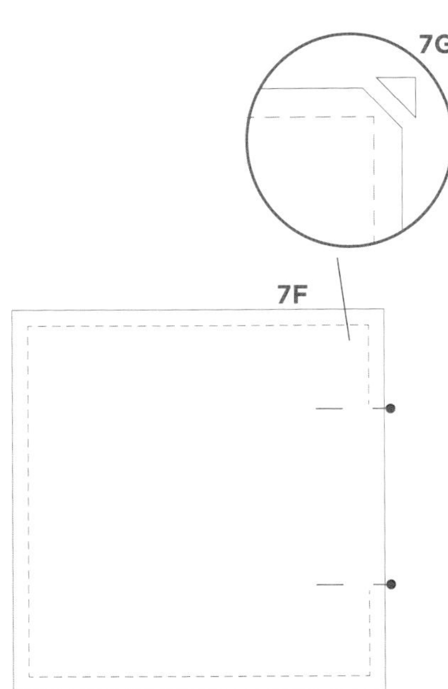

Turn right side out. Push the corners out. Press.

At the opening, turn the seam allowance to the inside and hold it taut as you press. This will give you a sewing line to use when you hand stitch the opening closed. Use Poly-Fil Fiber to stuff the pillow. Close the opening using an invisible hand stitch.

Fabric Checkerboard

King me! Stitch up a fun fabric checkerboard the whole family will love that includes storage for your pieces in clever zipper pouches. It can be used for portable games of chess as well. This fabric gameboard is quick and easy to make for your next gathering and travels well for road trips. Create this fun project and you've got game night in the bag.

MATERIALS

PROJECT SIZE
31″ x 21″

BLOCK SIZE
4½″ unfinished, 4″ finished

PROJECT SUPPLIES
1 package 5″ print squares
1 yard black - includes outer border, pockets, & binding

INNER BORDER
¼ yard or at least (2) 1¼″ strips

BACKING
¾ yard

OTHER
(2) 14″ zippers

**Note*: Add your own game pieces—you can even use buttons and coins!*

SAMPLE PROJECT
It's the Berries by Jill Finley for Riley Blake

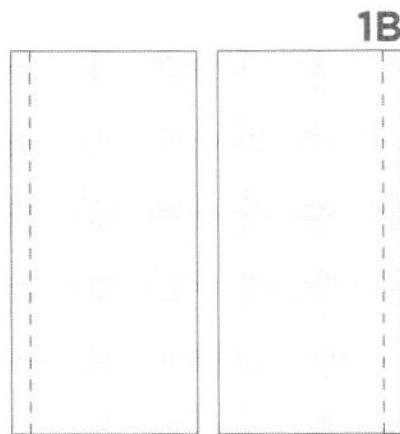

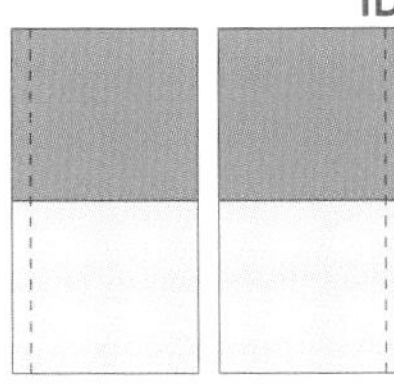

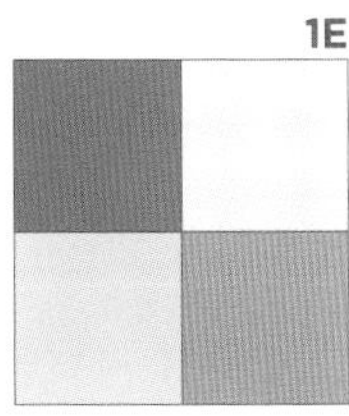

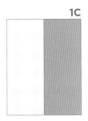

1 sort & sew

Select 8 light squares and 8 dark squares from your package of 5″ squares. Set the rest of the squares aside for another project.

Pick up a light square and a dark square and put them right sides together. Sew on opposite sides of the stacked squares. **Make 8**. **1A**

Cut the sewn squares in half between the seams 2½″ from either side. Press each unit toward the darker fabric. You will have 16 units. **1B 1C**

Select 2 non-matching units and lay them right sides together with the seam of each unit running horizontally. Nest the seams so that the light portion of the top unit is on top of the dark portion of the bottom unit. Sew on opposite sides of the stacked squares, crossing over your previously sewn seams. Cut the sewn units in half between the seams 2½″ from either side.

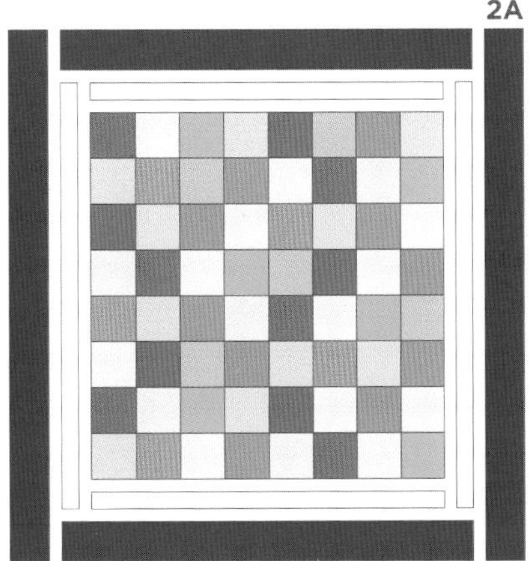

Press the seam allowance of each 4-patch toward 1 side. Repeat to **make (16)** 4-patch units. **1D 1E**

Block Size: 4½″ unfinished, 4″ finished

2 arrange & sew

Arrange your 4-patches in **4 rows** each made up of **(4) 4-patches**. Be sure to alternate between light and dark fabrics across your project and mix up the placement of the various prints. You can reference diagram **2A** as needed.

When you're happy with your arrangement, sew the 4-patches together in rows. Press the seams in opposite directions. Nest the seams and sew the rows together. Press again to complete the center of your project.

3 inner border

From the inner border fabric, cut (2) 1¼″ strips across the width of the fabric. Trim the inner borders from this strip.

Refer to Borders (pg. 118) in the Construction Basics to measure and cut the borders. The strips are approximately 16½″ for the top and bottom and approximately 18″ for the sides. Note that the borders on our project are sewn on the top and bottom of the project first, then along the sides.

4 outer border

From the black fabric, cut (2) 2¼″ strips across the width of the fabric. Trim the outer borders from this strip.

Refer to Borders (pg. 118) in the Construction Basics to measure and cut the borders. The strips are approximately 18″ for the top and bottom and approximately 21½″ for the sides. Note that the borders on our project are sewn on the top and bottom of the project first, then along the sides.

5 zippers

Note: You may need to switch the presser foot of your sewing machine to a zipper foot for this part of the project.

From the black fabric, cut a 1½″ strip across the width of the fabric. Set the rest of the fabric aside for now. Subcut (8) 1½″ x 4½″ rectangles from this strip.

Sandwich the non-separating end of a zipper in between (2) 1½″ x 4½″ black rectangles. The right sides of the fabric should be against the zipper. Pin in place.

Move the head of the zipper toward the middle of the zipper tape. Be sure the little stops on your zipper stay lined up and sandwich this second end of your zipper between (2) 1½″ x 4½″ black rectangles. Pin in place.

Sew across each sandwiched end of the zipper ¼″ from the edge, backstitching at each end of your seam. Go slow and be sure your needle will not run into the zipper stops. It is important to stitch as close to the zipper stops as possible to avoid having holes at the ends of your zippers. **5A**

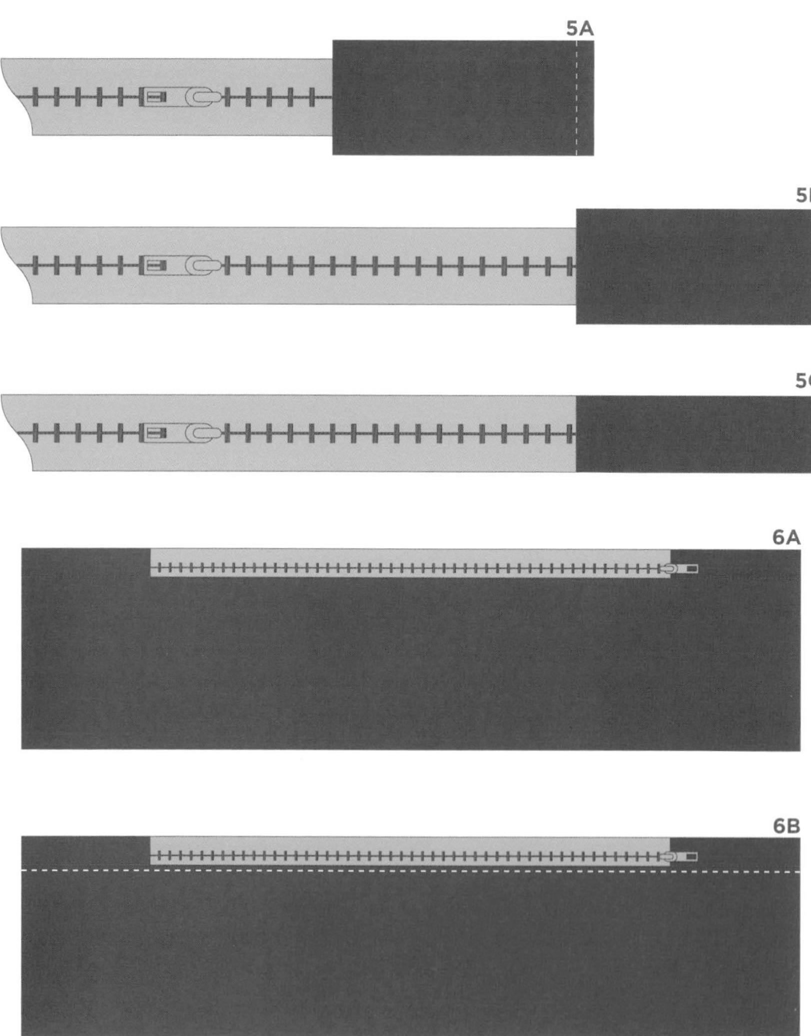

Fold the rectangles over the seams and press. **5B**

Trim the rectangles to the same width as your zipper. **5C**

Measure the size of your project and adjust the measurements listed as needed to match your project. Find the center of your zipper and measure out from this point in both directions. Cut the zipper approximately 10¾" from the center, so that it now measures 21½" in length. Repeat to make a second zipper.

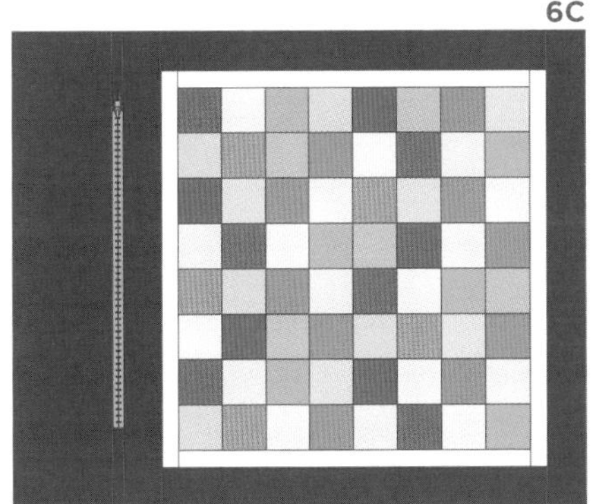
6C

6 make pockets

Note: Measure your project center and make any adjustments to the size of the pieces cut below as necessary.

From the black fabric:

- Cut (2) 5" strips across the width of the fabric. Subcut (2) 5" x 21½" rectangles from each of the strips.
- Cut (1) 6" strip across the width of the fabric. Subcut (2) 6" x 21½" rectangles from the strip.

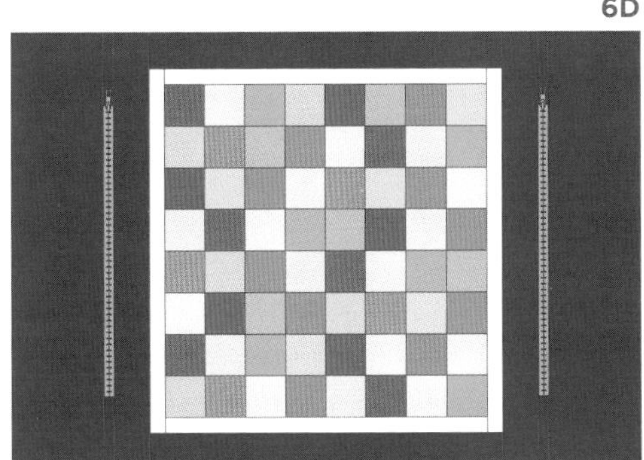
6D

Sandwich a zipper between (2) 5" x 21½" rectangles and pin in place. The right sides of the fabric should be touching the zipper. Sew along the top edge of the zipper using a zipper foot if necessary. When you get close to the zipper head, pause your sewing and move the zipper head past the presser foot and out of the way before finishing your seam. Fold the fabric rectangles back over the seam to expose the zipper and press in place. Press from both sides if necessary to get this as flat as possible. **6A**

Topstitch on the fabric along the zipper about ⅛" away from the seam. **Make 2**. **6B**

Lay the center of your project right side up with the longer borders on the left and right edges. Lay the pocket you just made on top of the project center with the unsewn side of the zipper aligned with the left side of the project center, right sides together. Lay a 6" x 21½" rectangle on top to sandwich the zipper and then pin in place. Sew along the edge. Fold back the fabric to expose the zipper and press just as you did before. **6C**

Repeat to create a pocket on the other side of the project. **6D**

After you have sewn both of the pockets to the project center to complete the top, use the top layer of the pocket as a guide to trim the layer underneath it.

7 quilt & bind

Layer the project with batting and backing and quilt. Be sure to keep your quilting between the zippers of the pockets and on the game board. You may also find it helpful to do a basting stitch around the perimeter of the project to hold the flaps of the pockets in place. After the quilting is complete, square up the project and trim away all excess batting and backing. Add binding to complete the project. See Construction Basics (pg. 118) for binding instructions.

Tree Farm Table Runner

Driving down country lanes past rows and rows of pine trees is always a welcome sight. These perfectly pruned beauties are getting ready for Christmas all year long! This darling quilt features rows and rows of cute little pine trees just like our favorite tree farm. And it's so easy to make with the new Missouri Star Large Wing template.

MATERIALS

PROJECT SIZE
53″ x 20″

BLOCK SIZE
6″ unfinished, 5½″ finished

PROJECT TOP
1 package 5″ print squares
1 yard of background fabric

BORDER
½ yard

BINDING
½ yard

BACKING
1¾ yards - vertical seam(s)

OTHER
Missouri Star Quilt Co.
Small Wing Template

SAMPLE PROJECT
Beautiful Day by Corey Yoder
for Moda Fabrics

1A

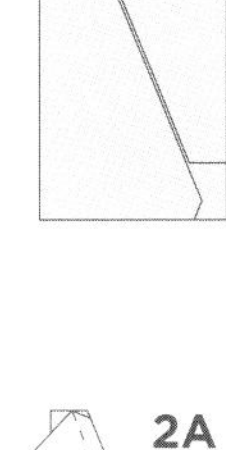

2A

2B

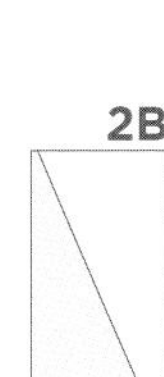

1 cut

Select at least (21) 5″ print squares and cut each selected square in half to yield 2½″ x 5″ rectangles. More squares can be used for added variety or to obtain the proper rotation on directional fabrics. **Note**: Pay attention to the prints on directional fabrics. These need to be cut vertically to ensure the print doesn't end sideways or upside-down.

Place the template upside-down in 1 corner of each rectangle and cut around the perimeter. Rotate the template 180° and place it in the opposite corner. Cut around the template again. You will need a **total of 81** print wings. **Note**: Depending on the exact size of your precut squares, you may have a hard time getting 2 wings from each rectangle. **1A**

From the background fabric:

- Cut (3) 5″ strips across the width of the fabric. Subcut a **total of (41)** 2½″ x 5″ rectangles from the strips. In the same manner as before, subcut a **total of 81** background wings from the rectangles.

- Cut (5) 2¼″ strips across the width of the fabric. Subcut 2¼″ x 6″ rectangles from the strips. You need a **total of (27)** 2¼″ x 6″ rectangles.

2 block construction

Lay a background wing on top of a print wing, right sides facing. Sew the 2 wings together. Open and press. **Make 81** units. **2A 2B**

Select 3 different units and sew them together in a row. Press. **Make 27** rows. If necessary, trim each row to 6″ x 4¼″. **2C**

Select 15 of the rows and sew a 2¼″ x 6″ background rectangle to the top of each row. Press. Trim to 6″ if necessary. **2D**

Select 12 of the rows and sew a 2¼″ x 6″ background rectangle to the bottom of each row. Press. Trim to 6″ if necessary. **2E**

Block Size: 6″ unfinished, 5½″ finished

3 arrange & sew

Refer to diagram **3A** on page 101 to arrange the blocks in **3 rows of 9**. Notice that each row starts with a block with the background rectangle along the top and alternates with the blocks with the background rectangle sewn to the bottom. When you are happy with your layout, sew the blocks together in rows. Press in opposite directions. Nest the seams and sew the rows together. Press.

1. Use the template to cut up to 2 wings from each 2½″ x 5″ print rectangle. Pay close attention to the orientation of any directional fabrics as you cut.

2. Place a background wing on top of a print wing, right sides facing. Align the slanted edges of the wings, then sew them together.

3. Open the unit and press the seam allowance towards the print fabric. Make 81 units.

4. Select 3 units with different print fabrics and sew them together to form a row as shown. Press, then trim to 6″ x 4¼″ if necessary. Make 27.

5. Sew a 2¼″ x 6″ background rectangle to the top of 15 rows. Press, then trim to 6″ if necessary.

6. Sew a 2¼″ x 6″ background rectangle to the bottom of 12 rows. Press, then trim to 6″ if necessary.

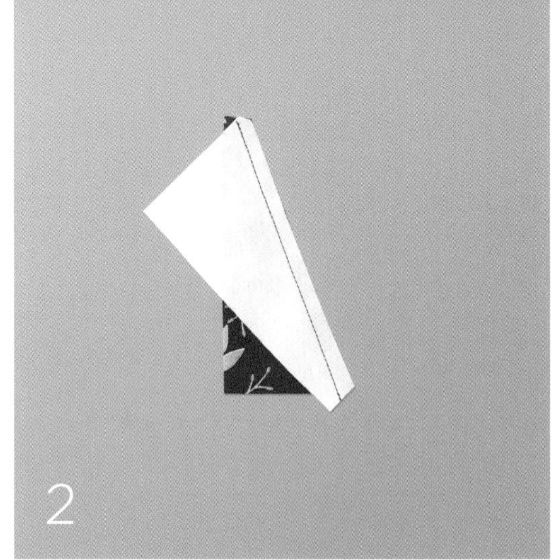

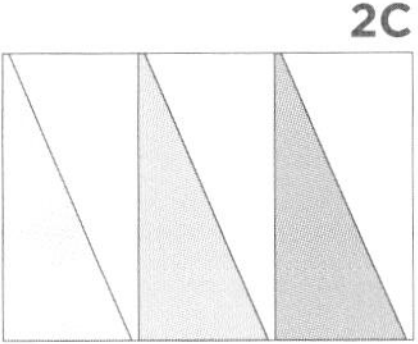

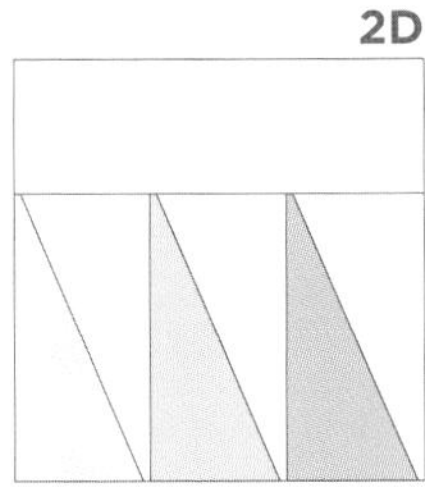

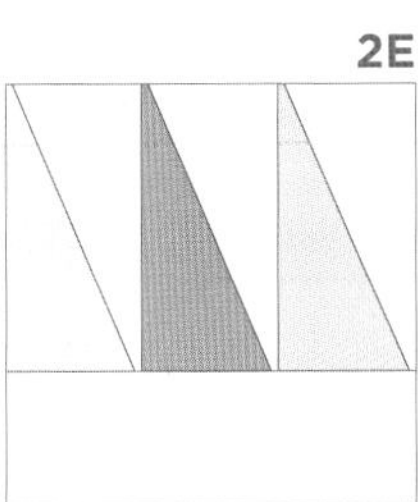

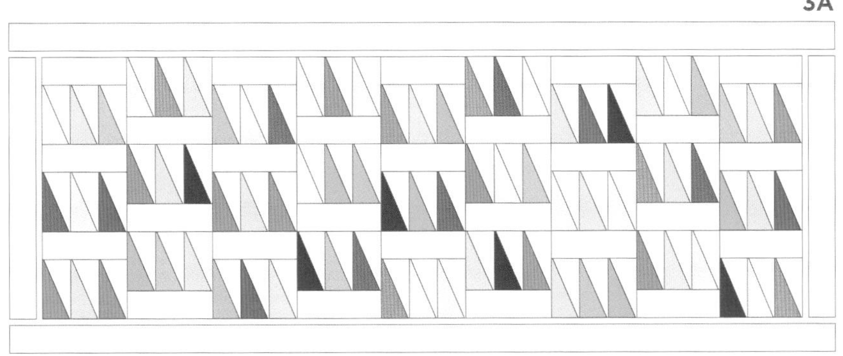

4 border

From the border fabric, cut (4) 2¼″ strips across the width of the fabric. Sew the strips together to make 1 long strip. Trim the borders from this strip. Refer to Borders (pg. 118) in the Construction Basics to measure, cut, and attach the borders. The lengths are approximately 17″ for the sides and 53½″ for the top and bottom.

5 quilt & bind

Layer the project with batting and backing, then quilt. After the quilting is complete, see Construction Basics (pg. 118) to add binding and finish your table runner.

Butterfly House

Build a darling butterfly house in your garden to attract the colorful creatures to your yard! These clever blocks are made with simple half-square triangles and a bit of sashing. Created with a kaleidoscope of fluttering patchwork butterflies, this charming Butterfly House quilt is sure to attract plenty of snuggles.

MATERIALS

QUILT SIZE
70½" x 87½"

BLOCK SIZES
- Butterfly - 9" unfinished, 8½" finished
- House - 9" x 26" unfinished, 8½" x 25½" finished

QUILT TOP
1 package of 10" print squares
½ yard of accent fabric
4¼ yards of background fabric

BORDER
1½ yards

BINDING
¾ yard

BACKING
5½ yards - vertical seam(s) or 2¾ yards of 108" wide

OTHER
Clearly Perfect Slotted Trimmer B - optional

SAMPLE QUILT
Fields of Gold by Lisa Audit for Wilmington Prints, **Wilmington Essentials Dry Brush Charcoal** by Wilmington Prints

1A

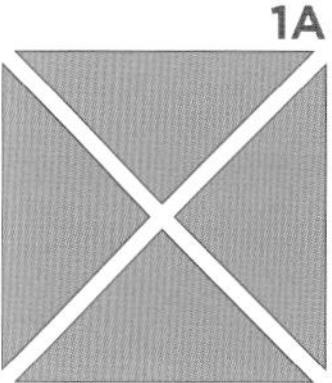

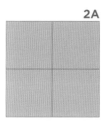

2A

2B

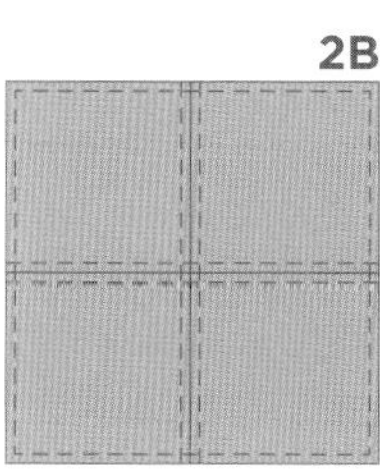

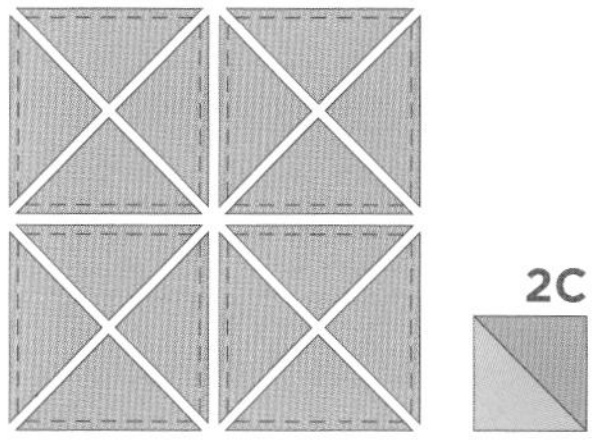

2C

2D

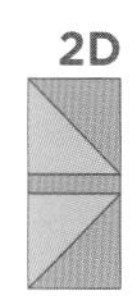

2E

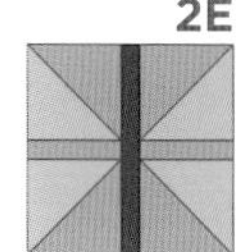

1 cut

From the accent fabric, cut (10) 1″ strips across the width of the fabric.

- From 9 strips, subcut a **total of (60)** 1″ x 6″ rectangles.

- Set the remaining strip aside for the house.

From the background fabric, cut:

- (4) 10″ strips across the width of the fabric. Subcut a **total of (15)** 10″ squares.

- (12) 8″ strips across the width of the fabric. Subcut a **total of (60)** 8″ squares. Subcut the squares twice on the diagonal. Each square will yield 4 setting triangles for a **total of 240**. **1A**

- (1) 5″ strip across the width of the fabric. Subcut (2) 5″ x 11½″ rectangles and set them aside for the house.

- (1) 4½″ strip across the width of the fabric. Subcut (1) 4½″ x 9½″ rectangle and (2) 4½″ x 9″ rectangles. Subcut the 4½″ x 9½″ rectangle into a **total of (2)** 2″ x 9½″ rectangles. Set the (2) 4½″ x 9″ rectangles and (2) 2″ x 9½″ rectangles aside for the house.

- (9) 1″ strips across the width of the fabric. Subcut a **total of (120)** 1″ x 3″ rectangles.

2 make the butterfly blocks

Select (15) 10″ print squares to use for the butterfly blocks. You may choose to make butterflies from additional squares for more variation. Select 2 matching 10″ print squares for the house. You can set any remaining print squares aside for another project.

Mark a horizontal and vertical centerline on the reverse side of each 10″ background square. **2A**

Layer a marked square with a print square, right sides facing. Sew around the perimeter of the squares using a ¼″ seam allowance. Sew on either side of both marked lines. **2B**

Cut on the marked lines, then cut each smaller sewn square on both diagonals. Use the trimmer to square each unit to 3″ then press open—or press, then square to 3″ if you're not using the trimmer. Each set of sewn squares will yield 16 half-square triangles. **2C**

Repeat with an additional (14) 10″ background and (14) 10″ print squares for a **total of 240** half-square triangles. Keep the matching units organized together.

Sew a half-square triangle to either side of a 1″ x 3″ background rectangle as shown. Press. **Make 2** matching units. **2D**

1. Cut on the marked lines, then cut each smaller sewn square on both diagonals. Square to 3″. Each set of sewn squares will yield 16 half-square triangles.
2. Sew a half-square triangle to either side of a 1″ x 3″ background rectangle as shown. Press. Make 2 matching units.
3. Sew the units just made to either side of a 1″ x 6″ accent strip as shown. Press. This butterfly unit should measure 6″ square.
4. Fold 4 setting triangles in half and press a crease to mark the center. Crease the centers along each edge of the butterfly unit. Match centers and sew a setting triangle to the top and bottom of the butterfly unit. Press.
5. Repeat to add a setting triangle to either side of the butterfly unit. Press. Square to 9″ if needed.

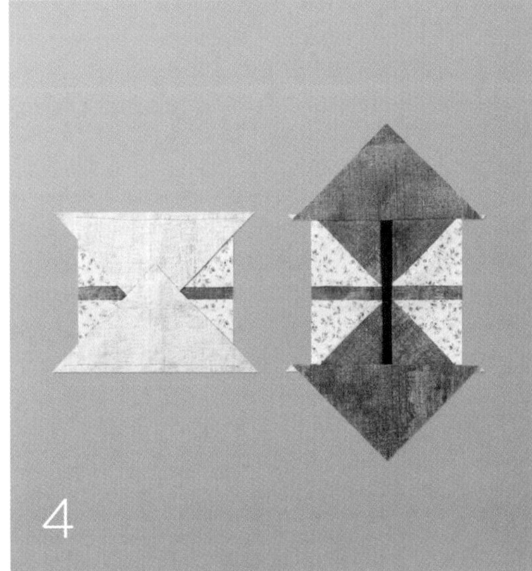

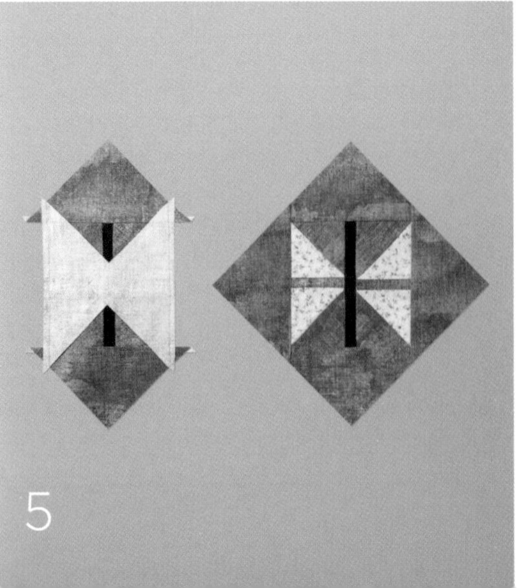

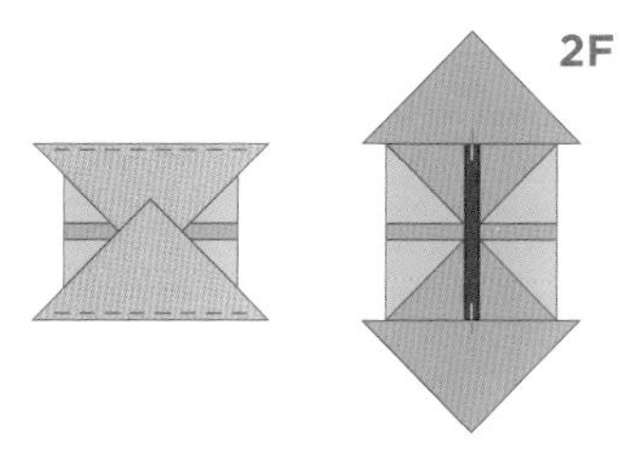

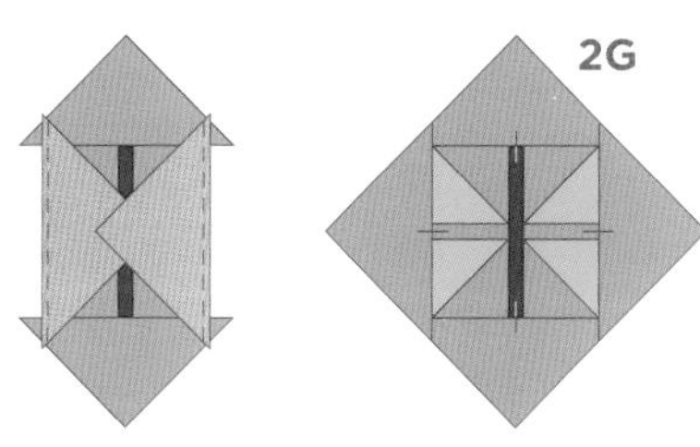

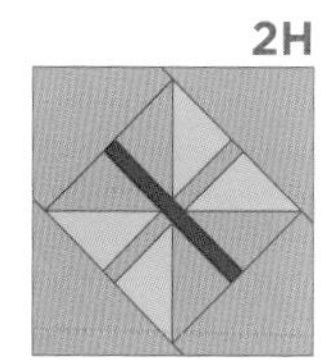

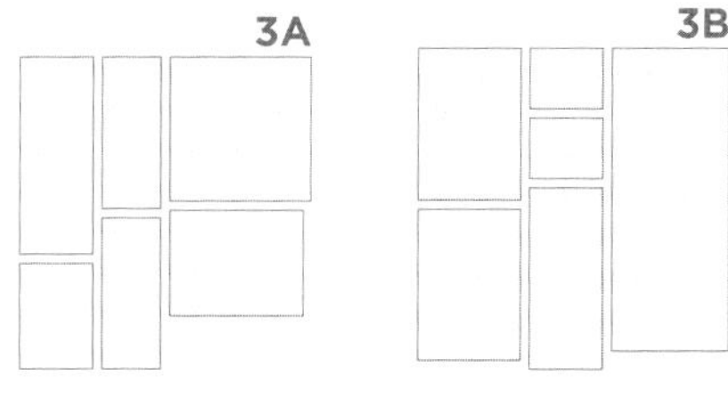

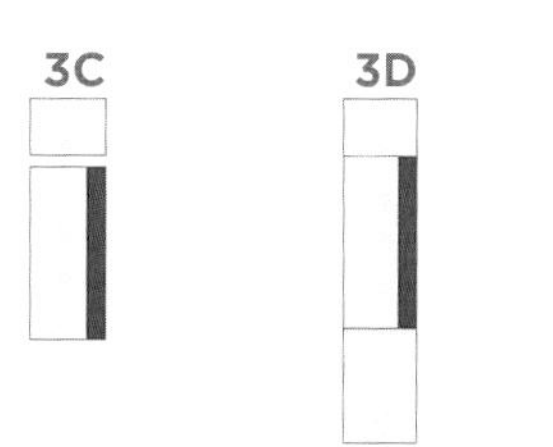

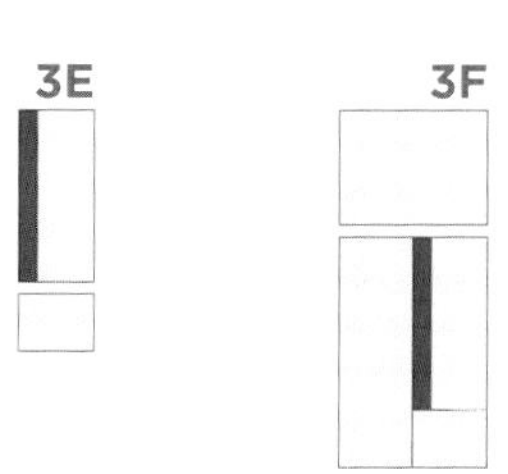

Sew the units just made to either side of a 1″ x 6″ accent strip as shown. Press. This butterfly unit should measure 6″ square. **2E**

Fold 4 setting triangles in half and finger press a crease to mark the center along the long edge. Repeat to fold and crease the centers along each edge of the butterfly unit. Match centers and sew a setting triangle to the top and bottom of the butterfly unit. Press. **2F**

Repeat to add a setting triangle to either side of the butterfly unit. Press. Square to 9″ if needed. **Make 60**. **2G 2H**

Butterfly Block Size:
9″ unfinished, 8½″ finished

3 make the house

Note: The cutting and assembly directions allow for the use of directional prints.
From the 2 matching 10″ print squares:

- Cut from 1 square:
  - (1) 2½″ strip along the *length* of the square. Subcut (1) 2½″ x 6½″ rectangle and (1) 2½″ x 3½″ rectangle.
  - (1) 2″ strip along the *length* of the square. Subcut (2) 2″ x 5″ rectangles.
  - (1) 4¾″ strip along the *length* of the square. Subcut (1) 4¾″ square. Trim the remaining piece to 4½″ x 3½″. **3A**
- Cut from 1 square:
  - (1) 3½″ strip along the *length* of the square. Subcut (2) 3½″ x 5″ rectangles.
  - (1) 2½″ strip along the *length* of the square. Subcut (2) 2½″ x 2″ rectangles.
  - Set the remaining pieces aside for another project. **3B**

You will have the following print pieces: (1) 2½″ x 6½″ rectangle, (2) 3½″ x 5″ rectangles, (1) 4½″ x 3½″ rectangle, (1) 4¾″ square, (2) 2″ x 5″ rectangles, (2) 2½″ x 2″ rectangles, and (1) 2½″ x 3½″ rectangle.

From the 1″ accent strip set aside earlier, cut (3) 1″ x 5″ rectangles and (2) 1″ x 13″ rectangles.

Sew a 2″ x 5″ print rectangle to the left side of a 1″ x 5″ accent rectangle as shown. Press. Sew a 2½″ x 2″ print rectangle to the top of the unit. Press. **3C**

Sew the 2½″ x 3½″ print rectangle to the bottom of the unit. Press. This bottom left unit should now measure 2½″ x 9½″. Set the unit aside for the moment. **3D**

Sew a 2″ x 5″ print rectangle to the right side of a 1″ x 5″ accent rectangle as shown. Press. Sew a 2½″ x 2″ print rectangle to the bottom of the unit. Press. **3E**

Sew the 2½″ x 6½″ print rectangle to the left side. Press. Sew the 4½″ x 3½″ print rectangle to the top. Press. This bottom right unit should now measure 4½″ x 9½″. **3F**

Sew the bottom left unit to the bottom right unit as shown. Press. Sew a 2″ x 9½″ background rectangle to either side of the bottom unit as shown. Press. Set this bottom unit aside for the moment. **3G**

Sew a 3½″ x 5″ print rectangle to either side of the remaining 1″ x 5″ accent rectangle as shown. Press. **3H**

Fold the 4¾″ print square in half and finger press a crease. Sew the square centered above the unit you just made. Press. Measure 3⅜″ in both directions from the center and make a mark along the bottom edge of the unit. Re-crease the top center of the unit if needed. Align your ruler edge with the top center crease and the mark on the bottom right, then trim along the edge of the ruler. Repeat to cut the left side. This is your roof unit. **3I**

Lay a 1″ x 13″ accent strip face down along the left edge of the roof unit, extending approximately ½″ past the bottom edge of the roof unit. Sew along the left edge using a ¼″ seam allowance. Press. **3J**

Repeat to add the second 1″ x 13″ accent strip to the opposite edge of the roof unit. Press. Trim the accent strips even with the bottom edge of the roof unit and along the angle of the strips at the top. **3K**

Lay a 5″ x 11½″ background rectangle along the left side of the roof unit, right sides facing, as shown. Align the top corner of the background piece with the tip of the roof unit. Sew along the left edge, then open and press. **3L**

Repeat to add the other 5″ x 11½″ background rectangle to the right side of the roof unit. **3M**

Measure ¼″ above the peak of the roof unit and trim across the top, parallel to the horizontal seam.

Trim the bottom even with the bottom edge of the roof unit. **3N**

Fold the bottom unit in half and finger press a crease along the top edge to mark the center. Center the roof unit to the top edge of the bottom unit. Pin as needed. Sew the units together and press. **Tip**: Lift the edge of your roof unit to make sure the print/accent seams will align with the print/background seams of the bottom house unit at ¼″ from the raw edges. Open and press. Recrease the center if needed. Measure 4½″ from the center and trim the unit to 9″ wide. **3O**

Sew a 4½″ x 9″ background rectangle to the top and bottom of the house. Press. Fold the unit in half, top to bottom, and finger press a crease to mark the center. Measure and trim the top and bottom 13″ from the center. **3P**

House Block Size:
9″ x 26″ unfinished, 8½″ x 25½″ finished

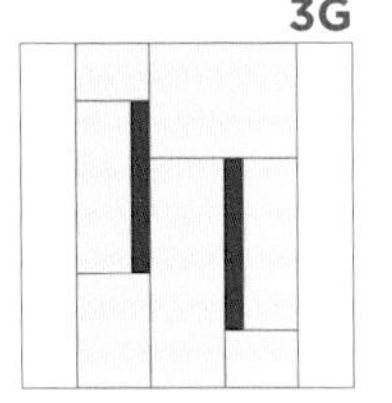
3G

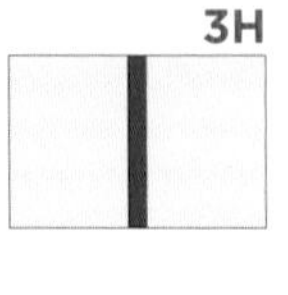
3H

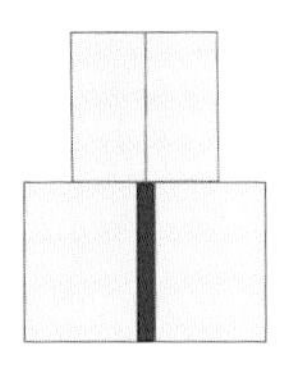
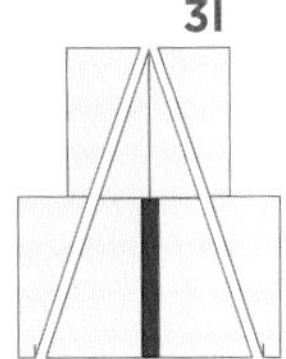
3I

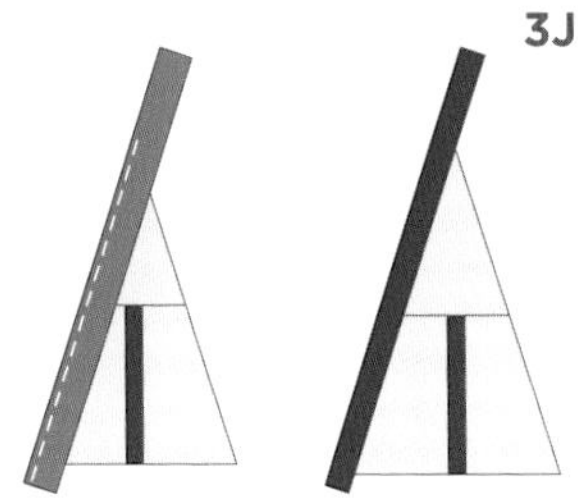
3J

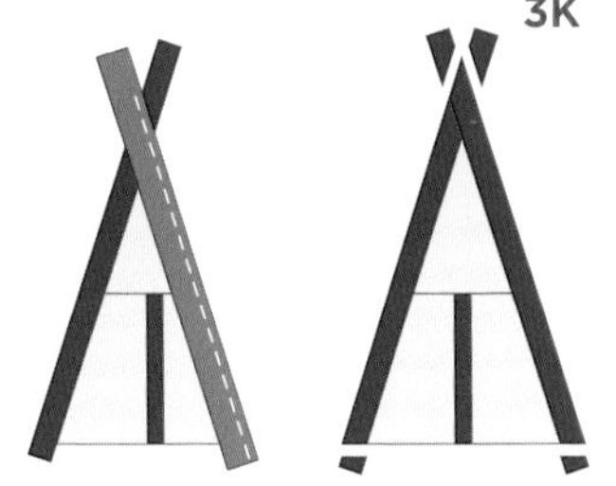
3K

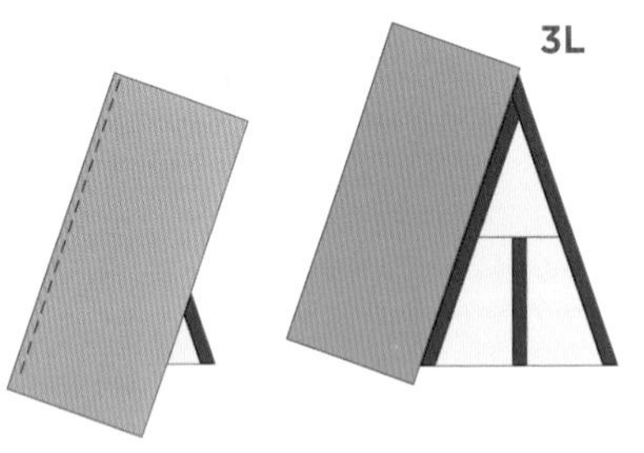
3L

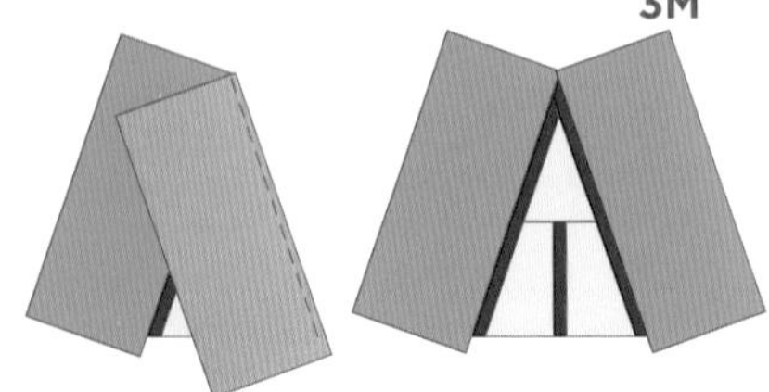
3M

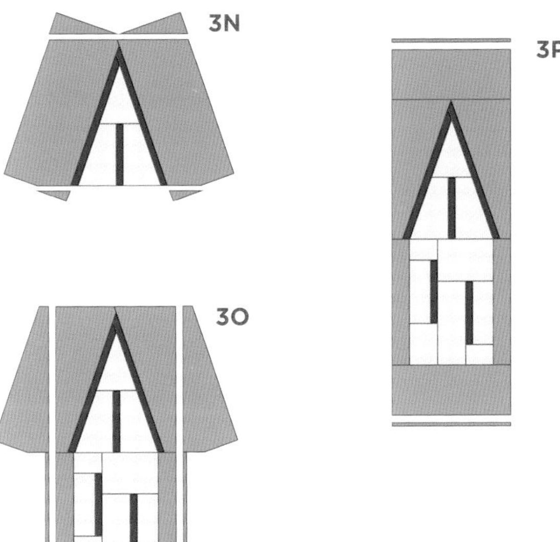

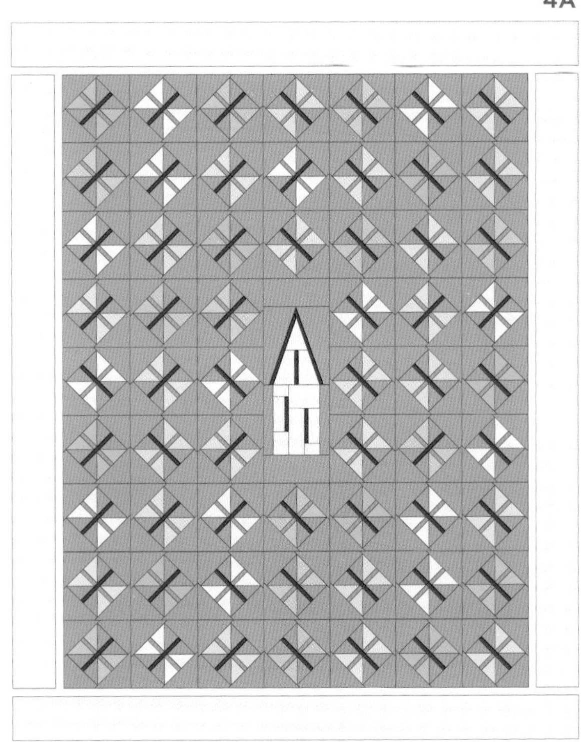

4 arrange & sew

Refer to diagram **4A** on the left to lay out your quilt as shown. Notice that the quilt is made up of **9 rows of 7**, but the house block takes the place of the 3 blocks in the center.

Sew the 9 blocks on the left side of the house together in rows and press in opposite directions. Nest the seams and sew the rows together. Press. Repeat with the other 9 blocks on the right side of the house. Sew these 9-block units to either side of the house block and press.
Sew the remaining blocks together in rows and press in opposite directions. Nest the seams and sew the rows together. Press.

5 border

Cut (8) 6″ strips across the width of the border fabric. Sew the strips together to make 1 long strip. Trim the borders from this strip. Refer to Borders (pg. 118) in the Construction Basics to measure, cut, and attach the borders. The lengths are approximately 77″ for the sides and 71″ for the top and bottom.

6 quilt & bind

Layer the quilt with batting and backing, then quilt. After the quilting is complete, see Construction Basics (pg. 118) to add binding and finish your quilt.

continued from page 49

Jenny took a deep breath. "Did you see the embroidery after you got your food?"

"Of course I did." Loretta stopped fluttering her hands around. "I'm not a fool. I checked on it as soon as I came back. She was at least two feet away talking to her husband."

Jenny leaned closer in an attempt to quiet the guild president. "And you still had the embroidery. So it wasn't her."

"But she left shortly after. She could have taken it while I was eating."

"So you did leave your bag alone?" Jenny asked patiently.

Loretta ruffled at the question and huffed at Jenny, "Of course not. I would never."

Jenny tried not to let her exasperation show while simultaneously looking for an escape. Her assistant's arrival across the park was the loophole she needed. "Look who's here. I'm going to go see if Cherry can help."

Loretta shot a disdainful look at Jenny. She ignored it, winding her way past an Irish Change quilt and a Disappearing Pinwheel in bright primary colors, before Jenny caught the younger woman who'd made herself indispensable. Cherry's strawberry blonde hair set off a turquoise blouse and a cardigan over a casual pair of fitted pink pants. Jenny smiled, knowing this was her casual look.

"Everything looks amazing! What did I miss?" Cherry's southern accent brightened the sunny sky and Jenny wrapped an arm around her shoulders.

"Not much. Just half the lunch. Oh, and Loretta lost a tablecloth so her world is falling apart."

Cherry pulled back from Jenny, her pinched brows displaying obvious confusion. After a brief explanation and a walk around the gathering, Cherry puckered her lips. "It's a little strange that it went missing. Has anyone made an announcement yet?"

Jenny shook her head. "Bernie's going to say something, but I'm sure it will turn up."

Just then Bernie's voice quieted the group and asked everyone to keep their eyes open for the vintage cloth.

"How terrible." A tall woman sidled up to Jenny and Cherry with a plate full of fruit in her hands. "That's not the piece Mrs. Manor had posted about on social media is it?"

A cough caught in Jenny's throat. "Social media?" It would be like Loretta to talk about her treasures trying to get people to come admire her.

"In a couple of places, I believe. It's actually why I came. I study vintage textiles and I have been anxious to see if hers holds up to its provenance." The woman held out her free hand. "I'm Amanda Jones."

Jenny led the way to one of the quilts and introduced herself and Cherry. "I'm so sorry you won't get to see Loretta's piece after all. According to her it was quite impressive. How long are you visiting?"

"Oh, I'm not visiting. My husband and I recently bought a place in town. With the growing fabric and quilting industry here it felt like the right place to be."

Cherry's jaw dropped and Jenny's excitement picked up. A vintage textile expert in town could be a boon to Hamilton's quilting industry.

"Well, let me know if there's anything we can do to help you settle in." Cherry said. "I'm no textile expert but I make a mean casserole."

Amanda laughed lightly, "thank you, but I feel terrible for Mrs. Manor. I'll have to keep my eyes open."

A chorus of ooh's and aah's sounded from the women around them and Jenny realized the Show and Tell portion of the meeting had begun. She glanced around and caught a very upset Loretta watching the group at large.

Jenny shook her head, "I'm sure she would appreciate that. It's hard to miss a six-foot by four foot white cloth dancing around the park."

It was Jenny's nature to try to keep people from worrying but it sounded ridiculous, even as she said it.

Amanda's face pinched, "Well, I didn't see any dancing cloths. And I didn't think much of it before, but I did see a blonde woman handing a decent sized white bundle to a man earlier."

"In the park?" Jenny tried to recall any men being there.

"Yes. He had curly hair and was a little scruffy. She handed him that bundle, and then they both disappeared. I haven't seen them since. Not that I know anyone, and I couldn't see them well, but I think they're gone." Amanda pushed herself up slightly though her height gave her an advantage over the crowd to begin with.

"Well, I'm still hoping it turns up but that's a start anyway." Jenny tugged at a thread hanging from the corner of her coat and had to force herself to leave it alone. Unthreading her jacket wouldn't help her understand what had happened.

Amanda chuckled. "You say that like a detective."

With a wink at Cherry Jenny shrugged. "It would be more helpful if I was. I'm just a quilter."

Jenny gave an awkward chuckle and Cherry gave a solid laugh.

"Okay," Amanda said, looking between them. Another round of applause sounded, catching the women's attention. As the sound died down Amanda stood. "It was wonderful to meet you. But I better be going."

They waved her off and Jenny bit her lip.

"Do you think someone might really have taken Loretta's embroidered tablecloth?" Cherry's question accented her tasting a finger full of frosting from a pale orange cupcake.

Jenny tipped her head to the side, "I was wondering the exact same thing. And that is our only lead."

Tracking down Amanda's address was a simple matter once the meeting was over. Loretta had gotten a sign-in of all the guests and with a little technology to look her up, Jenny and Cherry headed across town.

Jenny picked out the boxy three story home quickly. Not the most beautiful house on the street but it had potential. With its overgrown trees and deep-set placement along the street, it almost seemed like it was hiding.

As they approached, a loud crack splintered the air. Dust billowed in a cloud from the front of the Jones' home as the porch roof tumbled off the face of the house.

The car jerked to a stop and Jenny had her fist on the door handle staring out the window. "Did you see that?"

As the dust began to settle, the sound of boards cracking and breaking filled the air again and a figure dashed from the debris. A blue raincoat flaring out behind them.

"Hey!" Jenny called as the figure disappeared. It looked like they'd left something behind in the wreckage. Jenny jumped from the car followed by Cherry.

They ran to the porch and Jenny gasped as she saw a foot protruding from the rubble.

"Stop them!" She pointed after the escaping figure. Cherry didn't ask any questions. She zipped past Jenny, leaving her standing alone in the ruins of a friend's porch with a stranger's unmoving body.

to be continued...

REFERENCE

Boardwalk

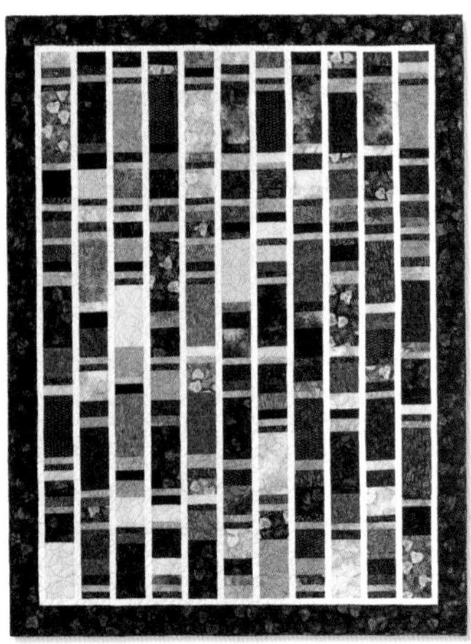

QUILT SIZE
70½″ x 94½″

BLOCK SIZES

- A - 5″ x 16″ unfinished, 4½″ x 15½″ finished
- B - 5″ x 7½″ unfinished, 4½″ x 7″ finished
- C - 5″ x 7½″ unfinished, 4½″ x 7″ finished
- D - 5″ x 10″ unfinished, 4½″ x 9½″ finished
- E - 5″ x 24½″ unfinished, 4½″ x 24″ finished
- F - 5″ x 12″ unfinished, 4½″ x 11½″ finished

QUILT TOP
1 package of 10″ print squares
1½ yards of coordinating print fabric
- includes outer border

¼ yard each of 3 different print fabrics
1 roll of 1½″ background strips
- includes sashing and inner border

BINDING
¾ yard

BACKING
5¾ yards - vertical seam(s) or 3 yards of 108″ wide

SAMPLE QUILT
Kasuri Artisan Batiks & **Artisan Batiks Magical Winter** by Lunn Studios for Robert Kaufman

QUILTING PATTERN
Arc Doodle

PATTERN
14

Layered Diamonds

QUILT SIZE
63″ x 60½″

BLOCK SIZE
8½″ x 7″ unfinished,
8″ x 6½″ finished

QUILT TOP
1 package of 10″ print squares
¼ yard each of 2 different accent fabrics

INNER BORDER
½ yard

OUTER BORDER
1¼ yards

BINDING
¾ yard

BACKING
4 yards – vertical seam(s) or 2 yards of 108″ wide

OTHER
Missouri Star Quilt Co. Large Wing Template
Missouri Star Large Simple Wedge Template for 10″ Squares

SAMPLE QUILT
Blue Breeze by Danhui Nai for Wilmington Prints

QUILTING PATTERN
Sticky Buns

PATTERN
22

Emotion Shadow Block

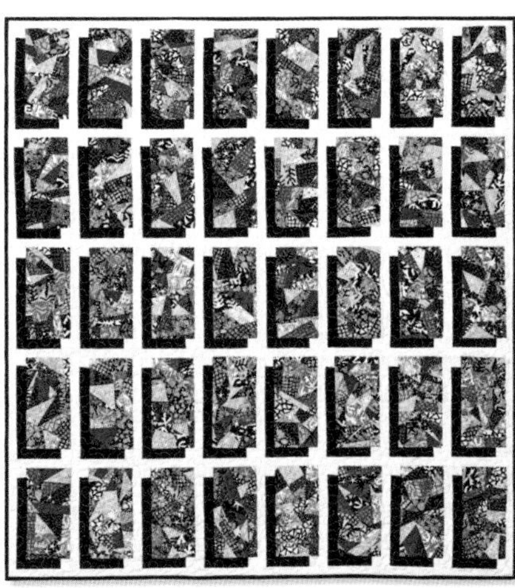

QUILT SIZE
53″ x 58½″

BLOCK SIZE
7″ x 12″ unfinished,
6½″ x 11½″ finished

QUILT TOP
1 roll of 2½″ print strips*
¾ yard of accent fabric
1 yard of background fabric - includes inner border

BINDING
½ yard

BACKING
3½ yards - horizontal seam(s)

**Scraps can be used to make crumb-pieced slabs if you prefer.*

SAMPLE QUILT
Sunkist Soleil and **Naturally Neutral Batik Solids - Cream** by Kathy Engle for Island Batik
Artisan Batiks Solids - Prisma Dyes Black by Lunn Studios for Robert Kaufman

PATTERN
34

Staccato Star Sew Along
Part 1

PRINT OUT YOUR OWN FABRIC KEY
msqc.co/staccato-star-fabric-key

BLOCK SUPPLIES - MORNING GLORY
(2) 10" fabric A squares
(1) 10" fabric B square
(1) 10" fabric C square
(1) 10" fabric D square
(1) 10" fabric F square
(1) 10" fabric H square
(2) 2½" fabric D strips

***Note**: Fabrics E, G, and I-N are not used in this block.*

BLOCK SUPPLIES - STUDIO STAR
(2) 10" fabric A squares
(3) 10" fabric B squares
(4) 10" fabric F squares
(4) 10" fabric G squares
(2) 10" fabric J squares
(3) 10" fabric L squares

***Notes**:*
- *Fabrics C, D, E, H, I, K, M, and N are not used in these blocks.*
- *We will be making dark and light versions of the Studio Star. We have kept the directions for each version separate to minimize confusion.*

TOTAL FABRIC REQUIRED IF YOU ARE SELECTING YOUR OWN:
Fabric A - ¾ yard
Fabric B - ¾ yard
Fabric C - ½ yard
Fabric D - ½ yard
Fabric E - 1 yard
Fabric F - 1¾ yards
Fabric G - 1¾ yards
Fabric H - 1 yard
Fabric I - 1 yard
Fabric J - 1 yard
Fabric K - ¾ yard
Fabric L - 2 yards
Fabric M - 1 yard
Fabric N - 1 yard

PATTERN
38

Just Wing It

QUILT SIZE
57" x 64"

BLOCK SIZE
7½" unfinished, 7" finished

QUILT TOP
1 package of 10" print squares

INNER BORDER
½ yard

OUTER BORDER
1¼ yards

BINDING
¾ yard

BACKING
3¾ yards or 2½ yards of 108" wide

OTHER
Missouri Star Quilt Co. Large Wing Template

SAMPLE QUILT
Fleurs by Michel Design Works for Northcott Fabrics

QUILTING PATTERN
Dragonfly

PATTERN
56

Lakeview Terrace

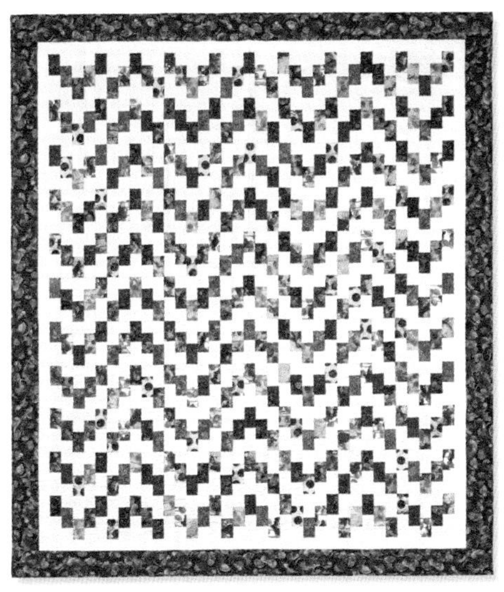

QUILT SIZE
83" x 95½"

BLOCK SIZE
10½" x 8" unfinished,
10" x 7½" finished

QUILT TOP
1 roll of 2½" print strips
4 yards of background fabric
- includes inner border

OUTER BORDER
1½ yards

BINDING
¾ yard

BACKING
8¾ yards - vertical seam(s)
or 3 yards of 108" wide

SAMPLE PROJECT
Modern Love by Deborah Edwards and Melanie Samra for Northcott

QUILTING PATTERN
Water

PATTERN
62

Lots O' Luck Table Runner

PROJECT SIZE
53" x 21"

BLOCK SIZE
16½" unfinished, 16" finished

PROJECT TOP
(2) 2½" strips or 1 fat quarter each of 4 different prints
½ yard of background fabric

BORDER
½ yard

BINDING
½ yard

BACKING
1¾ yards

SAMPLE PROJECT
Peacock Garden by Studio RK for Robert Kaufman

QUILTING PATTERN
Faster Posies

PATTERN
68

Conversation Heart Pillows

PRACTICE PDF SHEETS
msqc.co/handlettering

PROJECT SIZE
16" x 16"

PROJECT SUPPLIES
1 package of 5" solid or blender squares
½ yard of background fabric - includes pillow back

OTHER
Missouri Star Half-Heart Template
Missouri Star Fabric Markers
Missouri Star Light Fusible Adhesive 17" x 2 yards
PolyFil Fiber

BONUS - SMALL HEART PILLOWS

PROJECT SIZE
5½" x 5½"

PROJECT SUPPLIES
(1) 5" solid or blender square
¼ yard background fabric

OTHER
Missouri Star Half-Heart Template
Missouri Star Fabric Markers
Missouri Star Light Fusible Adhesive 17" x 2 yards*
PolyFil Fiber

**At least (1) 4¼" square of fusible adhesive is needed.*

PATTERN
84

Fabric Checkerboard

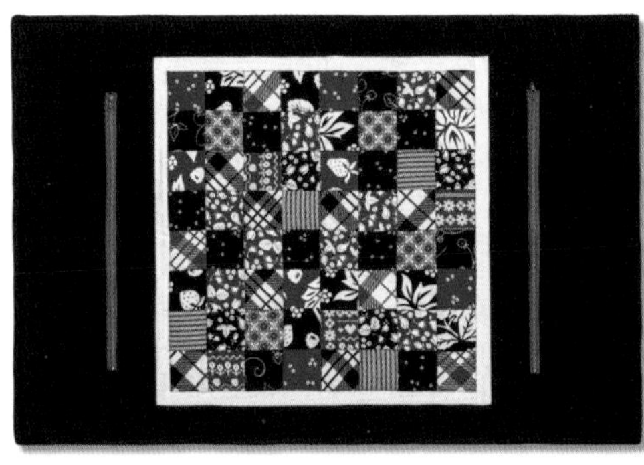

PROJECT SIZE
31" x 21"

BLOCK SIZE
4½" unfinished, 4" finished

PROJECT SUPPLIES
1 package 5" print squares
1 yard black - includes outer border, pockets, & binding

INNER BORDER
¼ yard or at least (2) 1¼" strips

BACKING
¾ yard

OTHER
(2) 14" zippers

*****Note**: Add your own game pieces - you can even use buttons and coins!*

SAMPLE PROJECT
It's the Berries by Jill Finley for Riley Blake

PATTERN
90

Tree Farm Table Runner

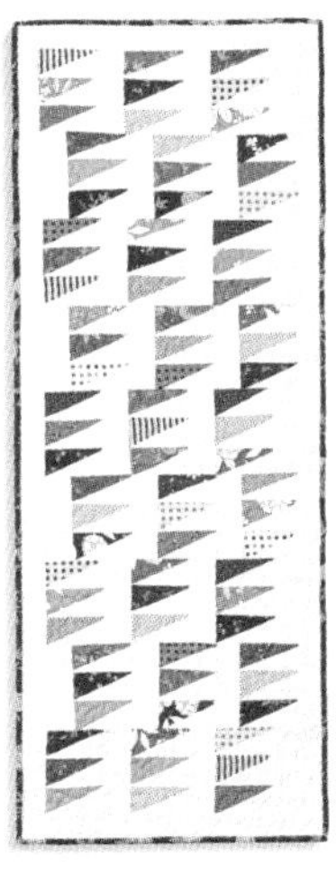

PROJECT SIZE
53″ x 20″

BLOCK SIZE
6″ unfinished, 5½″ finished

PROJECT TOP
1 package 5″ print squares
1 yard of background fabric

BORDER
½ yard

BINDING
½ yard

BACKING
1¾ yards - vertical seam(s)

OTHER
Missouri Star Quilt Co. Small Wing Template

SAMPLE PROJECT
Beautiful Day by Corey Yoder for Moda Fabrics

QUILTING PATTERN
Cotton Candy

PATTERN
96

Butterfly House

QUILT SIZE
70½″ x 87½″

BLOCK SIZES
- Butterfly - 9″ unfinished, 8½″ finished
- House - 9″ x 26″ unfinished, 8½″ x 25½″ finished

QUILT TOP
1 package of 10″ print squares
½ yard of accent fabric
4¼ yards of background fabric

BORDER
1½ yards

BINDING
¾ yard

BACKING
5½ yards - vertical seam(s) or 2¾ yards of 108″ wide

OTHER
Clearly Perfect Slotted Trimmer B - optional

SAMPLE QUILT
Fields of Gold by Lisa Audit for Wilmington Prints, **Wilmington Essentials Dry Brush Charcoal** by Wilmington Prints

QUILTING PATTERN
Flutterbyes

PATTERN
102

CONSTRUCTION BASICS

GENERAL QUILTING

- All seams are ¼" inch unless directions specify differently.
- Cutting instructions are given at the point when cutting is required.
- Precuts are not prewashed, therefore do not prewash other fabrics in the project.
- All strips are cut width of fabric.
- Remove all selvages.

PRESS SEAMS

- Use a steam iron on the cotton setting.
- Press the seam just as it was sewn right sides together. This "sets" the seam.
- With dark fabric on top, lift the dark fabric and press back.
- The seam allowance is pressed toward the dark side. Some patterns may direct otherwise for certain situations.
- Follow pressing arrows in the diagrams when indicated.
- Press toward borders. Pieced borders may need otherwise.
- Press diagonal seams open on binding to reduce bulk.

BORDERS

- Always measure the quilt top 3x before cutting borders.
- Start measuring about 4" in from each side and through the center vertically.
- Take the average of those 3 measurements.
- Cut 2 border strips to that size. Piece strips together if needed.
- Attach 1 to either side of the quilt.
- Position the border fabric on top as you sew. The feed dogs can act like rufflers. Having the border on top will prevent waviness and keep the quilt straight.
- Repeat this process for the top and bottom borders, measuring the width 3 times.
- Include the newly attached side borders in your measurements.
- Press toward the borders.

BINDING

find a video tutorial at: www.msqc.co/006

- Use 2½" strips for binding.
- Sew strips end-to-end into 1 long strip with diagonal seams, aka the plus sign method (next). Press the seams open.
- Fold in half lengthwise, wrong sides together, and press.
- The entire length should equal the outside dimension of the quilt plus 15" - 20."

PLUS SIGN METHOD

find a video tutorial at: www.msqc.co/001

- Lay 1 strip across the other as if to make a plus sign, right sides together.
- Sew from top inside to bottom outside corners crossing the intersections of fabric as you sew.
- Trim excess to ¼" seam allowance.
- Press seam open.

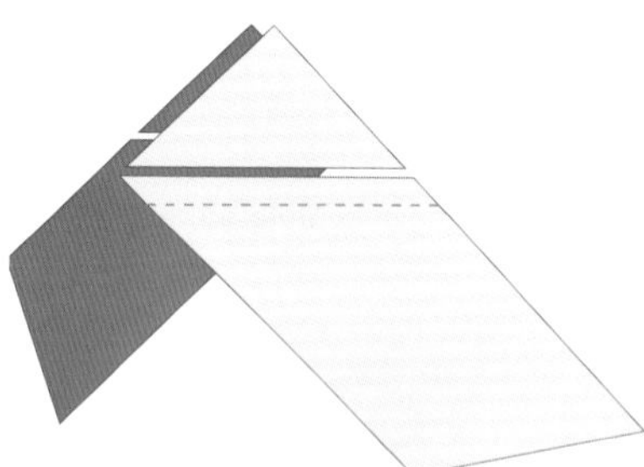

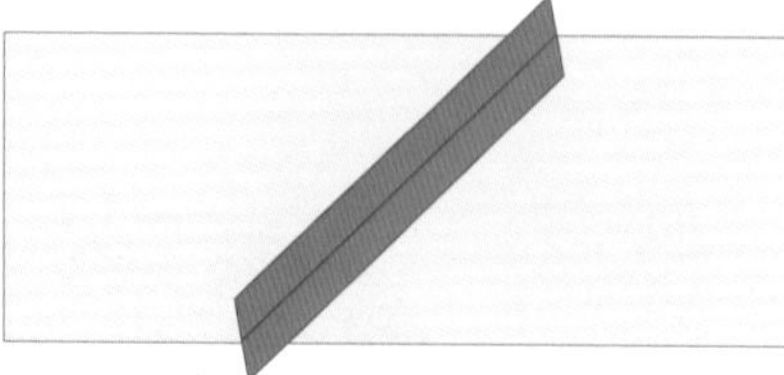

ATTACH BINDING

- Match raw edges of folded binding to the quilt top edge.
- Leave a 10" tail at the beginning.
- Use a ¼" seam allowance.
- Start in the middle of a long straight side.

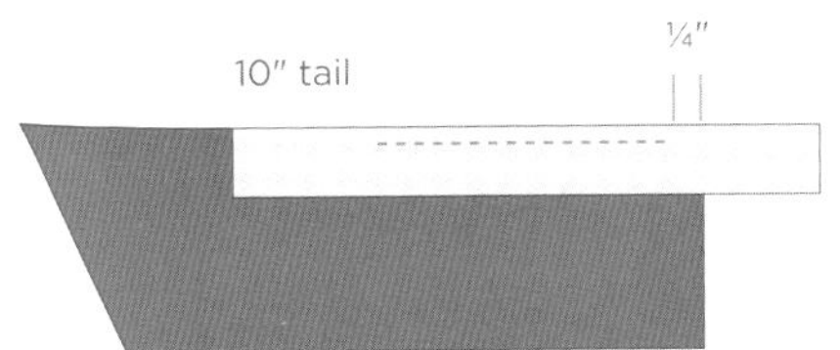

MITER CORNERS

- Stop sewing ¼" before the corner.
- Move the quilt out from under the presser foot.
- Clip the threads.
- Flip the binding up at a 90° angle to the edge just sewn.
- Fold the binding down along the next side to be sewn, aligning raw edges.
- The fold will lie along the edge just completed.
- Begin sewing on the fold.

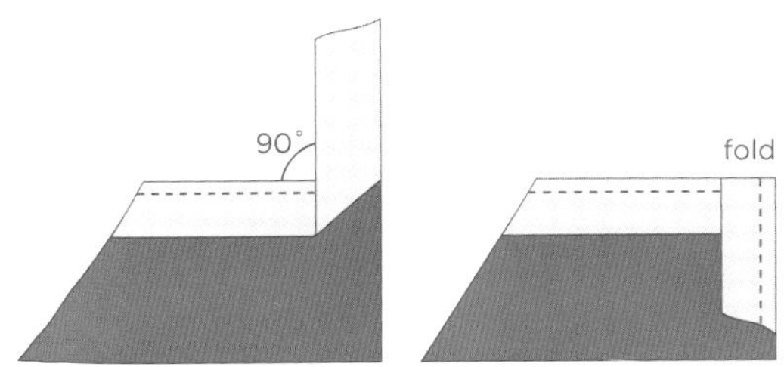

CLOSE BINDING

MSQC recommends The Binding Tool from TQM Products to finish binding perfectly every time.

- Stop sewing when you have 12" left to reach the start.
- Where the binding tails come together, trim the excess leaving only 2½" of overlap.
- It helps to pin or clip the quilt together at the 2 points where the binding starts and stops. This takes the pressure off of the binding tails while you work.
- Use the plus sign method to sew the 2 binding ends together, except this time when making the plus sign, match the edges. Using a pencil, mark your sewing line because you won't be able to see where the corners intersect. Sew across.

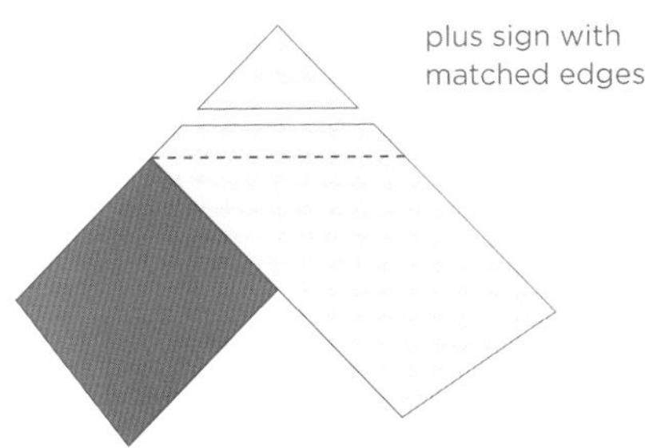

- Trim off the excess; press the seam open.
- Fold in half wrong sides together, and align all raw edges to the quilt top.
- Sew this last binding section to the quilt. Press.
- Turn the folded edge of the binding around to the back of the quilt and tack into place with an invisible stitch or machine stitch if you wish.